ISBN 978-1-330-47947-6
PIBN 10067301

1 MONTH OF
FREE
READING

at

www.ForgottenBooks.com

By purchasing this book you are eligible for one month membership to ForgottenBooks.com, giving you unlimited access to our entire collection of over 1,000,000 titles via our web site and mobile apps.

To claim your free month visit: www.forgottenbooks.com/free67301

English
Français
Deutsche
Italiano
Español
Português

www.forgottenbooks.com

Mythology Photography **Fiction**
Fishing Christianity **Art** Cooking
Essays Buddhism Freemasonry
Medicine **Biology** Music **Ancient
Egypt** Evolution Carpentry Physics
Dance Geology **Mathematics** Fitness
Shakespeare **Folklore** Yoga Marketing
Confidence Immortality Biographies
Poetry **Psychology** Witchcraft
Electronics Chemistry History **Law**
Accounting **Philosophy** Anthropology
Alchemy Drama Quantum Mechanics
Atheism Sexual Health **Ancient History**
Entrepreneurship Languages Sport
Paleontology Needlework Islam
Metaphysics Investment Archaeology
Parenting Statistics Criminology
Motivational

MAXWELL'S ENGLISH SERIES

WRITING IN ENGLISH

A MODERN SCHOOL COMPOSITION

BY

WILLIAM H. MAXWELL, M.A., Ph.D.

CITY SUPERINTENDENT OF SCHOOLS, CITY OF NEW YORK

AND

GEORGE J. SMITH, M.A., Ph.D.

MEMBER OF THE BOARD OF EXAMINERS, CITY OF NEW YORK

NEW YORK ∴ CINCINNATI ∴ CHICAGO

AMERICAN BOOK COMPANY

MAXWELL'S ENGLISH COURSE.

FIRST BOOK IN ENGLISH.
  For Use in Elementary Grades.

INTRODUCTORY LESSONS IN ENGLISH GRAMMAR.
  For Use in Grammar Grades.

ADVANCED LESSONS IN ENGLISH GRAMMAR.
  For Use in Higher Grammar Classes and in High Schools.

WRITING IN ENGLISH.
  For Use in Higher Grammar Classes and in High Schools.

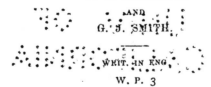

PREFACE

IT would doubtless be presumptuous to imagine that this book, as a guide to the preëminently important school subject of learning to write English, avoids all the faults of its predecessors, or contains more than a portion of their merits. But unless a text-book is thought to possess some definite advantages over the others in its field, it has no excuse for being. Attention is therefore directed to the following prominent features of this elementary treatise on *Writing in English :* —

1. The *general plan* of the development of the subject is noteworthy, as proceeding from the study and production of *entire compositions*, in the first chapters, to the study of the next order of composition-units, well-made *paragraphs*, then to *sentence-construction*, and, at length, to the smallest units of composition, *words.* Since it would, however, be unwise to complete any one of these great divisions of the subject before attending at all to the others, this general order, while it is kept in view throughout, is modified as shown in the Table of Contents; to which, and to its prefatory note, attention is requested. This plan is justified not only by the established principle of teaching from the whole to the parts, but by the experience of all able instructors in English, that nothing is more certain to kill a pupil's interest in composition than to compel him to begin the subject by laboring over the minutiæ of style and diction, as embodied in rules of good usage and exemplified in uncon-

3

266966

nected sentences. There should be composition, natural expression of connected ideas or observations, from the first. The study of the principles of sentence-construction and of choice of words should be made secondary, because the pupil does not perceive the value of such study to him, until, through the willing production of compositions expressing his own conceptions of life and nature, he has learned to feel the need of improving himself in the use of language. Interested observation and spontaneous thought require for their growth an atmosphere of freedom. Therefore it is that, in the early study of composition, we should aim, not at a finical remodeling of lay-figure sentences, but at copious and natural expression; and should defer a studied manipulation of sentences and of words until the student himself perceives the use of it. He must have something to say which he feels is worth saying and worth saying well. In this, as in other concerns, it is the spirit that giveth life, and it is the letter that killeth.

2. The method of studying *models* of good composition is prominent in this book. The number of extracts presented from good authors is large, and the character of them is such as to give of itself an interest and a value to the book. These selections are used as models not only of style, but of composition, — that is, of the skillfully ordered presentation of ideas. It is, in fact, as models of putting-together (composition) that they are first employed; the student's attention is primarily directed to the arrangement of their parts. Distinct from this use and yet along with it goes the employment of the selections as models for direct *imitation*. The effective influence of imitation in the molding of a good style is something that has been profited by, in schools, far too little. In support of it may be urged not only Dr. John-

son's advice, "to give days and nights to the study of Addison," and the recorded indebtedness of writers no less admirable than Irving and Robert Louis Stevenson to their conscious imitation of models, but, in fact, every person's unconscious response, in his own manner of writing, to the style of the authors he has read most and with most attention. The helpfulness of imitation is indeed one of the strongest bonds between the study of literature and the study of composition.

It may be well, before passing to the next heading, to direct attention also to the frequent employment, throughout the book, of the *inductive method* in the presentation of new points. It is strongly recommended that the teacher, by multiplying illustrations before calling for a principle, proceed in this method to a far greater extent than is possible in a text-book of strictly limited size.

3. Particular notice is directed to the great number and the practical character of the *exercises* in this book. They have been planned with great care, and their contents looked after no less sedulously than the order of their progression. It may fairly be said that the exercises constitute the active and living element in the book, — they should become, in the schoolroom, the outward form, concealing and vitalizing the skeleton-structure of the study.

In conclusion, a few words may be said regarding the *use of this book* by the teacher. Conditions vary so much in the myriad schools of this country, especially, perhaps, with regard to the study of English, that work adapted in many schools to the upper grammar grades may in others be precisely what is needed in the first year of the high school. It is difficult to present the principles of English composition simply enough to meet the understanding of children of grammar grades ; and in fact the cardinal

objection to nearly every composition text-book designed
for high-school use is that it presents the subject in a
manner too dry or too difficult for the average high-school
pupil.

Since the sensible teacher always regards a text-book
as a mere instrument, a means not an end, he will feel
free to omit, in his use of any book, whatever portions
seem either too difficult or otherwise ill adapted for his
particular class of pupils. He will, further, in order to
meet the needs of his pupils or to make the hard-and-fast
plan of a book flexible in use, deviate from its order of
exercises or even from its order of contents, as may seem
to him wise and good. Thus it would undoubtedly be
well to work at some of the chapters in this book two at
a time. Work in the sentence-making chapters (Chapters VI, VIII, etc.) might very well go on concurrently
with work in description, narration, or paragraphing. In
fact, the book will probably yield the best results if used,
to some extent, in this way. Nevertheless, the arrangement of the chapters and the progressive system of the
exercises are strongly recommended as a guide, in a general way, to the natural development of the subject ; and
they will, it is hoped, commend themselves, both in theory
and in practice, to all who use the book.

CONTENTS

NOTE TO TEACHERS. — Attention is asked to the remarks in the Preface, regarding the plan of this book. It is to be noted that the subject of composition is treated here under the following divisions: —

(a) Compositions, Chapters I, II, V, VII, XI, XIV.
(b) Paragraphing, Chapters III, IX.
(c) Sentence work, Chapters IV, VI, VIII, X, XII, XIII.

PAGE

PREFACE 3

CHAPTER

I. KINDS OF COMPOSITION 9
General Introduction (Exercises 1–4).
Narration, Description, etc., explained (Exercises 5–8 and Lists of Subjects).

II. STUDY OF DESCRIPTION 17
The Four Requisites in Good Composition (Exercises 9–12).
Planning and Outlining of Descriptions (Exercises 13–16).

PARAGRAPHING 37
Topics, Indention, Topic Sentences (Exercises 17–20).
Paragraph Making in Description (Exercises 21–25).

IV. UNITY IN SENTENCES (Exercises 26–30) 53

V. MORE ABOUT DESCRIPTION 60
Points of View; Use of Comparison.
Statement of Effects and of Sense Impressions (Exercises 31–41).

VI. SENTENCE FORMS 75
Kinds of Elements (Exercises 42, 43).
Kinds of Sentences and Transformations (Exercises 44–50).

VII. NARRATION 90
Outlining a Narrative (Exercises 51–56).
Construction of Narratives (Exercises 57–65).

CHAPTER		PAGE

VIII. CLEARNESS IN WRITING 111
Lack of Unity ; Omissions ; Misuse of Pronouns ; Misuse
of "which" ; Misplaced Modifiers (Exercises 66-71).

IX. CONTENTS OF PARAGRAPHS 121
Particulars ; Instances ; Comparisons ; Effects ; Reasons
(Exercises 72-85).

X. EMPHASIS IN WRITING 143
Forms of Sentences (Exercises 86-90).
Arrangement of Words (Exercises 91-97).
Choice of Words (Exercises 98-105).

XI. LETTER WRITING 162
Formal Notes, Informal Notes and Letters, Business
Letters (Exercises 106-112).

XII. FIGURES OF SPEECH (Exercises 113-121) 177

XIII. CHOICE OF WORDS 187
Correctness in Diction and Syntax (Exercises 122-128).
Choice in Diction : Use of Synonyms and of Suggestive
Words (Exercises 129-136).

XIV. EXPOSITION AND ARGUMENT. 206
Exposition (Exercises 137-139).
Argument (Exercises 140-146).

APPENDIX

I. MARKS FOR USE IN CRITICISM OF COMPOSITIONS . . 217

II. ENGLISH WORDS 221

III. RULES FOR PUNCTUATION, CAPITALIZATION, AND SPELLING
(Exercises 147-149) 232

IV. VERSES AND VERSE MAKING (Exercises 150-153) . . 244

V. NOTES ON AUTHORS REFERRED TO OR QUOTED IN THIS BOOK 259

INDEX 267

WRITING IN ENGLISH

CHAPTER I

KINDS OF COMPOSITION

THERE is hardly anything to be learned in school that is more important to us, all our lives, than how to talk and write properly and skillfully. We can see one reason for this, when we think how constantly all of us use language; and another reason occurs to us, when we think why it is that we ever say anything at all. We talk and write to let other people know what we have seen or thought or done, or to tell them what we wish them to do; and it is highly important to us that we accomplish these purposes.

But suppose, as it often happens, that those to whom we express ourselves fail to understand exactly what we are trying to tell them, or that they are not interested in what we have said. Then, of course, we should better have said nothing. There is no use in our writing at all, unless what we write has these two characteristics: First, *others must be made to understand our meaning*, readily and accurately; second, *what we say must be worth taking care to say well;* it must be *interesting*.

Now, in order that other persons may understand exactly what we mean to say, we must study how to form our *sentences* in the best possible ways, and how to put together our *compositions*. A good many of the chapters in this book tell about these matters, which, though they must be studied carefully, should nevertheless be interesting. For it is always interesting to learn how to do a thing well, and we should learn to think of our language as a very fine and a very wonderful tool or instrument which we wish to use skillfully. It is certainly worth much trouble to learn that. For think how a carpenter tries to get skill in the use of a chisel, or how the musician practices the playing of his violin. Language is an instrument both of use and of pleasure; we all of us employ it every day of our lives, and we may learn to get much enjoyment both from our own skillful use of it, and in appreciating the skillful use of it by others. Is it not really worth a great deal of study to learn to understand the masterly use of this instrument?

Then, as for *interesting* others in what we say, we would give this rule: The best way for you to be sure of interesting others is to write about what really interests *you*. Every one sees things, hears about things, does things that interest himself. These are, for each one of us, the very things we talk about or think about; they are what we should write about.

Exercise 1. Lists of subjects. — (*a*) *Make a list of the most interesting things you have ever seen, either near your home (as buildings, places, celebrations, etc.), or in* *school, or away from home.* (b) *Make a list of the most interesting things you now remember that ever happened to you or to any person you know very well (as journeys, excursions, outings, accidents, or the like).* (c) *Make a list of persons or objects you have heard of or read of and would like to learn more about.*

Exercise 2. Written review. — *Write a short statement of what has already been said in this chapter — why we make compositions, what we have to learn in studying composition, what we should write about, and why the study is important.*

Exercise 3. Punctuation. — *Look at all the punctuation marks so far used in this chapter, make a list of the different marks, and see if there are any places where a mark is used for no reason that you can see. If so, find out the reason from Appendix III, or from some person.*

Exercise 4. Spelling. — *Make a list of the words used so far in this chapter that you have sometimes misspelled, or have known some one else to misspell.*

Note concerning the exercises. — Each of the pupils should have a blank book and keep in it all the exercises which the teacher asks the class or the individual to write. The pages of the book should be numbered. In most cases the pupil should first write his answer or exercise on paper and correct it all he can before he copies it into the book. All the corrections made afterward should be made in *red ink*, so that the original writing can be easily seen by the pupil, the teacher, or any one else.

Do not be afraid that because of these corrections the book will not look neat. They show that you are learning something. Besides, if an exercise is much corrected, and if it is an important one, you can and should recopy it neatly in another part of the book, with all the improvements and corrections made. This should nearly always be done when the exercise is a *composition* that has been much corrected. Whenever you recopy an exercise, write at the end of the original the words, "Rewritten on page —." Reserve a page or two at the beginning of the book for a table of contents.

Compositions may be either written or oral, but when we think about what sorts of ideas we express, we find that either written or oral composition may be of four kinds. We are now going to divide compositions according to what we say in them.

The composition may be the story of what happened to somebody, really or in imagination; then it is called *narration*. Story books, histories, anecdotes, biographies, are all narratives, because they tell in some regular order what occurred or was done during a certain time. How you spent your last holiday, would be a subject of this sort. In the letters we write we often narrate happenings or events. There is at the end of this chapter a short list of subjects for narration.

Or what you wish to do may be to tell what some person or object or scene looks like, or what sort of person or thing it is. This kind of composition is called *description*. It tells the appearance and qualities of persons or objects. You can select many subjects for this kind of composition in the very room where you are sitting, and you can find many whenever you walk down the street or into the fields. Some subjects for description are given on page 15.

Sometimes we wish to show that a statement is true, or that it is false; and then we write or talk *argument.* Of course, when we argue the subject must always be a sentence, for it needs a sentence to state a truth or an untruth. A few subjects for argument are given on page 16.

Then, again, we may wish to explain a subject that interests us — to tell all we know about it. For example, suppose we take " Pencils." In writing upon a subject like this we should hardly *describe* pencils — there are too many kinds, and most of them would not be very interesting, for everybody knows what pencils look like; we should not have any *happening* to tell about, nor any statement to *argue* about; but if we knew, or could find out, how pencils are made, and where the lead comes from, and what different kinds of pencils there are, and so on, we might give some interesting information. Compositions of this sort, which explain and tell all about a subject, are called *expositions.* Most school books are expositions. A list of subjects for exposition is given on page 16.

Of course these four kinds of composition are not always kept separate. If you write about your last railway journey, you will probably tell what happened and also describe what you saw, and in your writing you have narration and description mingled. Nearly every story combines these two kinds of composition. In exposition and in argument, too, you will be very likely to have some description here and there, and perhaps some narration. But it is better to keep the four kinds of composition separate in your mind, so that at any rate you will know what you are doing. Besides, if we are to learn how to describe, and how to narrate, and so on, it will be much easier if, at first, we take up these kinds of writing one by one. So we shall begin Chapter II with description.

Exercise 5. Kinds of subjects. — *For what kinds of composition are the following subjects suitable?*
1. Flax. 2. A rain storm. 3. It is more agreeable to travel by steamboat than by railroad. 4. How paper is made. 5. Clouds. 6. The dandelion. 7. The story of the invention of the telegraph. 8. A morning walk. 9. Our school building. 10. The life of a butterfly.

Exercise 6. Kinds of subjects. — (a) *Taking the subjects you mentioned in Exercise 1, tell for what kinds of composition they are suitable. (b) What kind of composition was called for in Exercise 2?*

Exercise 7. Lists of subjects. — (a) *Write three amusing or odd subjects for description. (b) Write three subjects for accurate, careful description. (c) Write three subjects you have heard argued. (d) Write three interesting subjects for exposition, suggested by objects seen at home or at school or in street windows. (e) Write three subjects for narration.*

Exercise 8. Selections for copying or brief paraphrasing. — (a) *Find at home in a paper or magazine or book a good, brief description of a person or an object; bring it or a copy of it to school. (b) Find and copy an amusing or an interesting brief narrative, as an anecdote. (c) Tell the anecdote to the class at school. (d) Find and copy a brief piece of exposition or explanation. (e) Write a brief account of some argument you have heard or read, stating some of the reasons given as proofs.*

Brief Lists of Subjects

Note. — It is not intended that compositions should be written on any of these subjects at present. They are given here merely for further illustration of the different kinds of compositions.

I. *Description is the setting forth of the appearances and qualities of persons or objects.*

1. My dog. 2. The way our grandfathers dressed. 3. A house fly under a magnifying glass. 4. An odd visitor. 5. An old-time mansion. 6. A strange old lady. 7. A portrait. 8. A scene in the country (a picture). 9. The Angelus (a picture). 10. Our schoolhouse (outside view). 11. My room at home. 12. A secondhand bookstore. 13. A striking show window. 14. The first railway train. 15. The fire last Thursday night. 16. An old piece of furniture. 17. A certain tree. 18. View in the park. 19. What I heard and saw in the woods. 20. A successful newsboy.

II. *Narration is the setting forth in some intended order of real or imaginary connected happenings.*

1. An incident observed in a street car. 2. Account of a ball game. 3. The events of a Saturday excursion. 4. My last railway journey. 5. The story of a poor boy.. 6. How Ethel helped support her mother. 7. An amusing incident. 8. A trip by water. 9. A ghost story. 10. A theft, and how the thief was caught. 11. How I spent my Christmas vacation. 12. An unpleasant evening. 13. A ramble down Broadway. 14. The adventures of a lucky boy. 15. The life of William Shakspere. 16. The story of coal. 17. The history of the adoption of our national flag. 18. The future histories of our classmates. 19. A hunting adventure. 20. A day on the farm.

III. *Exposition, or explanatory composition, is the setting forth of the nature and relations of a substance, a class of objects, or an idea.*

1. How food is digested. 2. Earthworms. 3. How baseball is played. 4. Birds of prey. 5. Why spring comes. 6. The value of geography. 7. What is courage? 8. How a boat is sailed. 9. The making of a book. 10. An education for business life. 11. Timepieces. 12. Precious stones. 13. How paper is made. 14. How a knight was educated. 15. The circulation of the blood.

IV. *Argument is the setting forth of proofs or disproofs of a proposition, and the overthrowing of proofs offered by one's opponents.*

1. Arithmetic is less useful than geography. 2. Should the law forbid the sale of intoxicating drinks? 3. The United States should not retain the Philippines. 4. Athletics in school should be encouraged. 5. Capital punishment should not be used. 6. Does higher education fit one for business life? 7. Should education be compulsory? 8. Is war ever right? 9. Lowell was a greater poet than Longfellow. 10. It is sometimes wise for workmen to strike.

CHAPTER II

WHAT is the object in writing descriptions? When we understand what people write descriptions for, we may learn in what respects we need skill, or what things we must see to when we write. Our aim in describing anything is to let others know how it impresses us — what it is, as we see it — and to cause others to see it in imagination, and to feel about it as we do. Now we cannot possibly tell all there is to be observed in even a small object. For instance, we could not clearly tell in words about all the spots and markings, the colors, and the exact shape in minutest detail, of a single apple. When we describe anything, therefore, we must select only those points that seem to us worth mentioning, the things that strike us and that we wish our readers to see and feel. We must also keep to the subject, so as to avoid confusing our readers; but, on the other hand, we must not leave out anything that ought to be mentioned. Finally, we must arrange the points of our description skillfully, so as to make what we say interesting, and so as to produce on our readers a clear impression.

In good descriptions, therefore (and the same is true of all good compositions and, indeed, of all good works of art), will be found these four qualities: 1, *skillful selection;* 2, *unity;* 3, *completeness;* 4, *plan.*

Selection implies that the writer has a purpose in view, and that he chooses, from all that he might mention, those particular points that are interesting and important for his purpose. This purpose may be merely to give full and accurate information (as in the description of the starfish on page 30); or it may be to entertain; or, more usually, it is to produce an emotional effect upon the reader, that is, to cause the reader to feel as the writer wishes him to feel.

Unity requires that the writer shall not wander from his subject; that is, that he shall not bring in anything which is foreign to the subject. If you were describing a house, and should break off in the midst of your description, to tell of some events that happened in the house, perhaps years before, you would be forgetting the principle of unity. Unity means oneness; each composition must be a well-made whole.

Completeness requires that nothing necessary or important be omitted. If you were describing a man's face, and should say nothing of his eyes or of his expression, your description would lack completeness.

The requirement of *plan* simply means that a writer must say what he has to say, in some well-thought-out order or arrangement of the parts. Plan is fully as important as selection, unity, or completeness, and we shall have to study very carefully how to plan well all that we write.

Now let us read and consider the following description of a scene in a court room. In London, the judge (called here the " Lord Chancellor ") and the lawyers (called " gentlemen of the bar ") wear gray wigs and silken gowns. This description was written by Charles Dickens : —:

The High Court of Chancery. (From *Bleak House,* by Charles Dickens, Ch. XXIV.)

When we came to the Court, there was the Lord Chancellor sitting in great state and gravity, on the bench, with the mace and seals on a red table below him, and an immense flat nosegay, like a little garden, which scented the whole 2 Court. Below the table, again, was a long row of solicitors, with bundles of papers on the matting at their feet; and then there were the gentlemen of the bar in wigs and gowns — some awake and some asleep, and one talking and 3 no one paying much attention to what he said. The Lord Chancellor leaned back in his very easy chair, with his elbow on the cushioned arm, and his forehead resting on his hand; some of those who were present dozed; some read the newspapers; some walked about, or whispered in groups : all seemed perfectly at their ease, by no means in a hurry, very unconcerned, and extremely comfortable.

Now mark, in the first place, that Dickens by no means tells all that he might have told about this court scene. There were, no doubt, many details to be seen that he does not mention. You could not, from this description, form an entirely clear mental

picture of the place, or make a plan or map of the
court room. He *selects* the points that suit his purpose. This purpose is to make you feel what an indif-
ferent, unfeeling, machinelike thing the court was.
The care and worry and sorrow of the persons whose
affairs were disposed of there, seemed to be nothing
to those drowsy and extremely comfortable officials.

In the second place, the description is a *unit;* not
one thing is mentioned that has not to do with the
scene described.

In the third place, this description, though brief,
is *complete* enough to include all that helps out the
purpose in view. There we see the persons present,
how they are placed in the room, and what they are
all doing; and we see the most striking objects in
the room, the easy chair of the Chancellor, the table,
the mace[1] and the seals, the newspapers, the lawyers'
papers, and the bouquet.

Finally, the *plan* of the description is very clear
and excellent. Our attention is first directed to
the figure a visitor would naturally observe in the
first glance, that of the presiding judge, the Lord
Chancellor. The first sentence describes briefly the
general appearance of the Chancellor, and tells of
the objects near him. The other persons present are
then mentioned, with their surroundings (sentence 2).
Then the third sentence tells what the various persons present, from the Lord Chancellor down, are
doing. The plan might be stated thus: —

[1] Look up "mace" in the dictionary.

1. Situation of the persons and objects observed.
2. Occupations of the persons.

Exercise 9. Study of the qualities of descriptions. —
(a) *In a similar way study the following . descriptions with regard to their selected details, their unity, their completeness, and their plan.* (1) *Ask yourself what the general impression is that the writer wishes to produce, and note the points selected for the purpose;* (2) *note whether the writer keeps to the business in hand and avoids speaking of things that have no sufficient connection with the subject;* (3) *note whether each description mentions everything we should naturally wish to know about the subject; and* (4) *note whether there is a well-defined plan.* (b) *Then write down the subjects of the parts of each description, in the order in which the parts appear.*

The Kitchen of an English Inn. (From *The Sketch Book*, by Washington Irving; paper on *The Stage Coach.*)

As we drove into the great gateway of the inn, I saw on one side the light of a rousing kitchen fire beaming through a window. I entered and admired, for the hundredth time, that picture of convenience, neatness, and broad honest enjoyment, the kitchen of an English inn. It was of spacious dimensions, hung round with copper and tin vessels highly polished, and decorated here and there with a Christmas green. Hams, tongues, and flitches of bacon were suspended from the ceiling; a smokejack made its ceaseless clanking beside the fireplace, and a clock ticked in one corner. A well-scoured deal table extended along one side of the kitchen, with a cold round of beef and other hearty viands upon it, over which two foaming tankards of ale seemed mounting guard. Travelers of inferior order were preparing to attack this stout repast, while others sat smoking and gossiping over their ale on two high-backed oaken settles beside the fire. Trim housemaids were hurrying backward and forward under the directions of a fresh, bustling landlady; but still seizing an occasional moment to exchange a flippant word and have a rallying laugh with the group round the fire.

Holden's House after the Rains. (From *Without Benefit of Clergy,* by Rudyard Kipling.)

He found that the rains had torn down the mud pillars of the gateway, and the heavy wooden gate that had guarded his life hung drunkenly from one hinge. There was grass three inches high in the courtyard; Pir Khan's lodge was empty, and the sodden thatch sagged between the beams. A gray squirrel was in possession of the veranda, as if the house had been untenanted for thirty years instead of three days. Ameera's mother had removed everything except some mildewed matting. The *tick-tick* of the little scorpions as they hurried across the floor was the only sound in the house. Ameera's room and that other one where Tota had lived were heavy with mildew; and the narrow staircase leading to the roof was streaked and stained with rain-borne mud. Holden saw all these things and came out again.

Jo. (From *Little Women,* by Miss L. M. Alcott, Ch. I. ˙Little, Brown, and Company, by permission.)

Fifteen-year old Jo was very tall, thin, and brown, and reminded one of a colt; for she never seemed to know what to do with her long limbs, which were very much in her way. She had a decided mouth, a comical nose, and sharp, gray eyes, which appeared to see everything, and were by turns fierce, funny, or thoughtful. Her long, thick hair was her one beauty; but it was usually bundled into a net to be out of her way. Round shoulders had Jo, big hands and feet, a fly-away look to her clothes, and the uncomfortable appearance of a girl who was rapidly shooting up into a woman, and didn't like it.

Exercise 10. Reproductions. — (*a*) *Read over again, carefully, twice, Irving's description of the big kitchen of the inn; then take your list (see Exercise 9, b) of points mentioned in the several sentences, and write out from memory what Irving says.*[1] *In doing this, try to keep very close to his way of writing, imitate his choice of words and his formation of sentences. See how nearly like Irving you can write.* (*b*) *Give the same description orally.*

Exercise 11. Imitation of model. — *Now select some similar subject for description, a scene in a restaurant, or a hotel, or a sitting room, with a number of people in it, variously occupied. Then, with Irving's description open before you, write your description, as nearly as possible in the manner of Irving.*

[1] Although the rules for the use of capitals and of punctuation marks are given in the appendix, a few of the most important are printed here, to serve as a reminder : —

Capitals should be used to mark —

The first word of a sentence, or of a line of poetry.

The first word of a somewhat long quotation ; as, *John replied*, " *The man then, after*," etc.

Proper names, titles, names of the Deity.

The pronoun I, and the interjections O, Oh.

Periods should be used to mark —

The close of all sentences, except direct questions (?) or exclamatory sentences (!).

Abbreviations ; as, *T. A. Kerley, M.D.; Mon., Aug. 7, etc.*

Commas mark most of the natural pauses in sentences, and are used particularly —

After nouns of address ; as, *John, come here.*

After words in a list or series, where " and " or " or " is omitted.

Before and after explanatory or thrown-in words, phrases, or clauses.

The pupil should avoid using slang words. If there is any doubt as to a word's being good English, look it up in the dictionary.

Exercise 12.   Imitation of model. — *Take for a subject some old ruined or deserted house, or a shanty; study carefully Mr. Kipling's description of Holden's house; note the plan; then write an imitation of his description, but using your own subject.*

Now a further study of the descriptions already given will help us in learning *how to plan* our own compositions.

We observe first that in beginning the description each of the writers quoted tells us what first catches the attention, gives us, as it were, the effect of a single *glance*.   Then he goes on to mention the important details in some regular order.   To have a regular order, he must group the details under well-marked *divisions*.   Now, to see to these matters properly, we must think out our plan beforehand. To have a good plan in a description or in any other kind of composition is very important; there can be no excellent description without it.   Most persons cannot make good plans for their compositions while they are writing; the plan should always be made beforehand.   No builder would set to work on a house till the plan was decided upon; so no good writing can be done without a similar attention to plan.   Writing down the scheme or plan of a composition is called *outlining*.   To make outlines before writing not only leads us to form a good plan, but it helps us to secure both completeness and unity in the points selected for our composition.

The study of the descriptions already given may

teach us the following points about the outlining of descriptions : —

1. We may or may not have an *introduction* to our description. In the selections given from Dickens and from Mr. Kipling the description begins at once. In the selection from Irving the first sentence may be called introductory; it is the second that takes us with the writer into the inn kitchen.

2. The *description* begins with a *glance;* what would be naturally noticed first of all is mentioned first and briefly, with a statement of the impression it makes. Thus the glance view strikes, as it were, the key-note of the whole description.

3. In the *detailed description* which follows, and which makes up most of the body of the description, the writer proceeds according to some definite plan by means of dividing the subject into *parts* or *features*, arranging these in what seems the best order, and then giving such details or particulars under each division as aid in producing the effect desired.

This is illustrated in the following selection : —

Description of Bleak House. (From *Bleak House*, by Charles Dickens, Ch. VI.)

1 It was one of those delightfully irregular houses where you go up and down steps out of one room into another, and where you come upon more rooms when you think you have seen all there are, and where there is a bountiful provision of little halls and passages, and where you find still older cottage rooms in unexpected places, with lattice windows
2 and green growth pressing through them. Mine, which we entered first, was of this kind, with an up-and-down roof,

that had more corners in it than I ever counted afterward, and a chimney (there was a wood fire on the hearth), paved all around with pure white tiles, in every one of which a

3 bright miniature of the fire was blazing. Out of this room you went down two steps, into a charming little sitting room,

4 looking down upon a flower garden. Out of this you went up three steps into Ada's bedroom, which had a fine broad

5 window, commanding a beautiful view. Out of this room, you passed into a little gallery with which the other best rooms (only two) communicated, and so, by a little stair-

6 case of shallow steps, down into the hall. But if, instead of going out at Ada's door, you came back into my room, and went out at the door by which you had entered it, and turned up a few crooked steps that turned off in an unexpected manner from the stairs, you lost yourself in passages, with mangles in them, and three-cornered tables, and a Native-Hindoo chair, which was also a sofa, a box, and a bedstead, and looked in every form something between a bamboo skeleton and a great bird cage, and had been brought from India nobody knew by whom or when.

7 From there you came on Richard's room, which was part library, part sitting room, part bedroom, and seemed indeed

8 a comfortable compound of many rooms. Out of that you went straight, with a little interval of passage, to the plain room where Mr. Jarndyce slept, all the year round, with his window open, his bedstead without any furniture stand- ing in the middle of the floor for more air, and his cold bath

9 gaping for him in a smaller room adjoining. Out of that, you came into another passage where there were back stairs, and where you could hear the horses being rubbed down, outside the stable, and being told to Hold up, and Get over, as they slipped about very much on the uneven stones.

10 Or you might, if you came out at another door (every room had at least two doors), go straight down to the hall again by half a dozen steps and a low archway, wondering how you ever got back, or had ever got out of it.

The plan of this description may be expressed in the following outline : —

I. Glance — Delightful irregularity of Bleak House, illustrated in its arrangement of rooms and passages

II. Detailed description
   a. The first circuit to the hall
      1. My room
         a. Its roof
         b. The fireplace
      2. The sitting room, how you reached it, and what you saw from its window
      3. Ada's bedroom
      4. The gallery and stairway to the hall
   b. The second circuit
      1. The passages from the other side of my room
         a. Mangles and tables
         b. The Indian chair
      2. Richard's room
      3. Mr. Jarndyce's bedroom
         a. Open window
         b. Bedstead
         c. Cold bath
      4. Passage near the stable
         a. Stairs
         b. Stable sounds heard
      5. Stairway to the hall

Let us now take a description of a person, and outline it : —

Description of Mr. Hyde. (From *Dr. Jekyll and Mr. Hyde,* by Robert Louis Stevenson, p. 58.)

I had never set eyes on him before, so much was certain. He was small, as I have said; I was struck besides with the shocking expression of his face, with his remarkable combination of great muscular activity and great apparent debility of constitution.

This person (who had, from the first moment of his entrance, struck in me what I can only describe as a disgustful curiosity) was dressed in a fashion that would have made an ordinary person laughable; his clothes, that is to say, although they were of rich and sober fabric, were enormously too large for him in every measurement, — the trousers hanging on his legs and rolled up to keep them from the ground, the waist of the coat below his haunches, and the collar sprawling wide upon his shoulders. Strange to relate, this ludicrous accouterment was far from moving me to laughter. Rather, as there was something abnormal and misbegotten in the very essence of the creature that now faced me — something seizing, surprising, and revolting — this fresh disparity seemed but to fit in with and to reinforce it; so that to my interest in the man's nature and character there was added a curiosity as to his origin, his life, his fortune, and status in the world.

I. Glance

    a. The man's strangeness to me

    b. Stature

    c. Expression of face

    d. Bodily characteristics

II. Detailed description

   a. The man's clothes

      1. Quality of material

      2. Size

         trousers

         coat

   b. Impression made by the man

      1. Sense of surprise and revolt

      2. Sense of curiosity

Exercise 13. Outlining of description. — *In a similar manner make written outlines of the following descriptions:* —

Description of David Gamut. (From *The Last of the Mohicans*, by James Fenimore Cooper, Ch. I.)

The person of this individual was to the last degree ungainly, without being in any particular manner deformed. He had all the bones and joints of other men, without any of their proportions. . . . His head was large; his shoulders narrow; his arms long and dangling, while his hands were small, if not delicate. His legs and thighs were thin, nearly to emaciation, but of extraordinary length; and his knees would have been considered tremendous had they not been outdone by his feet. The ill-assorted and injudicious attire of the individual only served to render his awkwardness more conspicuous. A sky-blue coat, with short and broad skirts and low cape, exposed a long thin neck and longer and thinner legs. His nether garment was of yellow nankeen, closely fitted to the shape, and tied at his bunches of knees with large knots of white ribbon, a good deal sullied by use. Clouded cotton stockings, and shoes, on one of the latter of which was

a plated spur, completed the costume of the lower extremity
of this figure. From beneath the flap of an enormous pocket
of a soiled vest of embossed silk, heavily ornamented with
tarnished silver lace, projected his musical instrument. A
large civil cocked hat, like those worn by clergymen within
the last thirty years, surmounted the whole, furnishing dignity
to a good-natured and somewhat vacant countenance.

Description of the Starfish. (From *Life on the Seashore,* by
J. H. Emerton, p. 59.)

The starfishes are among the most peculiar animals of the
seashore, and belong to a class, the Echinoderms, others of which
live on land or in fresh water. The common starfishes live
near low water mark, coming above it occasionally, and in
winter retreating to deep water. They live on mollusks, and
are a great nuisance to the oyster growers. They fold themselves around an oyster or mussel, turn their stomach out of
their mouth and in between the shells of the bivalve and
digest it without taking it inside their bodies. The starfishes
move by suckers in the fine grooves on the under side of their
arms. To bring them into use they have to be filled with water
from the water tubes, which receive their supply from the
porous colored spot on the back of the starfish and carry it
through all the arms, giving off a branch to each sucker.

The skin of the starfish is filled with little hard plates and
from it project spines of various shapes. These spines have,
around the base, clusters of little organs which have jaws that
open and shut, for no apparent purpose unless to prevent dirt
from sticking to the skin. At the end of each arm is an eye.

Description of a Street Pageant. (From *Varia,* by Agnes Repplier, p. 114. Houghton, Mifflin, and Company, by permission.)

Suddenly there came the sound of drums playing a gay and
martial air, and in another minute, surrounded by a clamorous
mob, the Sire de Gayant and his family moved slowly into
sight.

Thirty feet high was the Sire de Gayant, and his nodding plumes overtopped the humble roofs by which he passed. His steel breastplate glittered in the evening sun; his mighty mace looked like a May-pole; his countenance was grave and stern. The human pygmies by his side betrayed their insignificance at every step. They ran backward and forward, making all the foolish noises they could. They rode on hobby-horses. They played ridiculous antics. They were but children, after all, gamboling irresponsibly at the feet of their own Titanic toy. Behind the Sire de Gayant came his wife, in brocaded gown, with imposing farthingale and stomacher. Pearls wreathed her hair and fell on her massive bosom. Earrings a handbreadth in size hung from her ears, and a fan as big as a fire screen was held lightly by a silver chain. Like Lady Corysande, " her approaching mien was full of majesty;" yet she looked affable and condescending, too, as befitted a dame of parts and noble birth. Her children manifested in their bearing more of pride and less of dignity. There was even something theatrical in the velvet cap and swinging cloak of her only son; and Mademoiselle Gayant held her head erect in conscious complacency, while her long brown ringlets fluttered in the breeze.

Happily, however, there was still another member of this ancient family, more popular and more well beloved than all the rest, Mademoiselle Thérèse, " la petite Binbin," who for two hundred years has been the friend and idol of every child in Douai. A sprightly and attractive little girl was Mademoiselle Thérèse, barely eight feet high, and wearing a round cap and spotless pinafore. In her hand she carried a paper windmill. She ran hither and thither with uncertain footsteps, pausing now and then to curtsy prettily to some admiring friends in a doorway; and whenever the pressure of the crowd stopped her progress, the little children clamored to be held up in their fathers' arms to kiss her round, smooth cheeks. One by one they were lifted in the air, and one by one I saw them put their arms around la Binbin's neck, and embrace her so

A Viking

heartily that I wondered how she kept herself clean and un-crumpled amid these manifold caresses.

Description of the Mansion of Tully-Veolan, from the inner courtyard. (From Scott's *Waverley*, Ch. VIII.)

The house, which seemed to consist of two or three high, narrow, and steep-roofed buildings, projecting from each other at right angles, formed one side of the inclosure. It had been built at a period when castles were no longer necessary, and when the Scottish architects had not yet acquired the art of designing a domestic residence. The windows were numberless, but very small; the roof had some nondescript kind of projections, called bartizans, and displayed at each frequent angle a small turret, rather resembling a pepper box than a Gothic watchtower. Neither did the front indicate absolute security from danger. There were loopholes for musketry, and iron stanchions on the lower windows, probably to repel any roving band of gypsies. . . . Stables and other offices occupied another side of the square. The former were low vaults, with narrow slits instead of windows. . . . Above these dungeon-looking stables were granaries, called girnels, and other offices, to which there was access by outside stairs of heavy masonry. Two battlemented walls, one of which faced the avenue, and the other divided the court from the garden, completed the inclosure.

The Burning of Rome, A. D. 64. (From *The Early Days of Christianity*, by Canon F. W. Farrar, Book I, Ch. IV.)

But the sense of permanent loss was overwhelmed at first by the immediate confusion and agony of the scene. Amid the sheets of flame that roared on every side under their dense canopy of smoke, the shrieks of terrified women and the wail of infants and children were heard above the crash of falling houses. The incendiary fires seemed to be bursting forth in so many directions, that men stood staring in stupefaction at the destruction of their property or rushed hither and thither in

helpless amazement.   The lanes and valleys were blocked up
with the concourse of struggling fugitives.   Many were suffo-
cated by the smoke, or trampled down in the press.   Many
others were burnt to death in their own burning houses, some
of whom purposely flung themselves into the flames in the
depth of their despair.   The density of the population that
found shelter in the huge many-storied lodging houses increased the difficulty of escape; and when they had escaped
with bare life, a vast multitude of homeless, shivering, hungry
human beings — many of them bereaved of their nearest and
dearest relatives, many of them personally injured, and most of
them deprived of their possessions, and destitute of the means
of subsistence — found themselves huddled together in vacant
places in one vast brotherhood of hopeless wretchedness.

Exercise 14.   Description from picture. — *Observe the
picture of the Viking (page 32) carefully, make a brief
but well-arranged list of the points in it that should be
mentioned, then write the description after the manner
of Cooper's description of David Gamut.*

Exercise 15.   Description from picture. — *After observing carefully what is represented in the picture on
page 35, prepare an outline for a description of it, then
describe it, orally or in writing, from your outline.*

Exercise 16.   Outline and original description. — *(a) Bring
into the class an outline for a description, by yourself,
of some person seen on the street, or elsewhere. Select a
more or less peculiar-looking person, whom you may see
and observe before working up your description. Descriptions from memory are apt to be vague and scanty,
or else inaccurate.*

*(b) Write the description of the person, following the
outline made. This outline should already be in. the
exercise book. When writing the composition, leave a
margin of one inch at the left.*

QUEEN ELIZABETH AND RALEIGH

Note to teachers. — All the written exercises of the pupils should be inspected at intervals by the teacher, and a certain proportion of the original compositions should be carefully read and criticised by the teacher, who should note in the margin the points wherein the pupil is to correct or improve. There is a list of marks for criticism given in Appendix I. The teacher will at first have to use only such marks of criticism as the pupils are ready to profit by. As the study continues, more and more of the marks may be employed. The compositions that have been criticised by the teacher should be corrected by the pupil in red ink, between the lines, and then shown again to the teacher. If the changes made are satisfactory, and the composition is an important one, it should be rewritten in the same book.

An important aim with the teacher, however, should be to teach each pupil to criticise and improve *his own work.* As the study advances, the pupil should become more and more able, by the help of the text-book and the instructions of the teacher, to criticise his own writing with certainty, correctness, and even pleasure. Of course the points in which the pupil is to criticise his work should at first be few and simple. They may progressively increase in number and difficulty, but the teacher should always afford the pupils in this all possible guidance and assistance. Nor can the teacher's own direct criticism of some proportion of the compositions ever be entirely dispensed with, though the ideal to be worked toward is the pupil's well-instructed but independent and self-helping criticism.

CHAPTER III

PARAGRAPHING

WHEN we write descriptions, or other compositions of considerable length, they are often or generally clearer and easier to read if in some way it is made plain where one part or division ends and the next begins. For this reason, compositions are almost always divided into parts or sections called *paragraphs*. The beginning of a paragraph is marked by placing the first word of it a little to the right of where the lines of writing or print regularly begin. This setting of a word to the right of the other first words of the lines is called *indention*. The word " when " at the beginning of this paragraph is indented. If you turn to page 12 in this book, you will see the paragraphs all marked by indentions. The words " The," " Or," " Sometimes," " Then," and so on, are indented, because they begin new paragraphs.

Now, since each paragraph stands for a distinct part of the plan of a composition, it has a distinct subject of its own. This subject is called the *topic* of the paragraph.

In the following description there are, as the indentions show, five paragraphs. The *topics* of them may be stated and subdivided thus : —

1. The scene in the garret (including "introduction" and "glance")
   a. Dimness of the place (introduction)
   b. The white-haired shoemaker (glance view)

2. The old man's voice

3. His appearance
   a. Tools, etc., about him
   b. His face
      white beard and hair
      hollow cheeks
      unnaturally bright eyes
   c. His clothing
      shirt
      other garments

4. Special features of the man
   a. His thin hands
   b. His vacant gaze
   c. His habit of wandering in attention

5. His absent-mindedness
   a. Unconscious movements
   b. Difficulty of arousing him

The Shoemaker of the Bastille. (From *A Tale of Two Cities*,
by Charles Dickens, Ch. VI.)

The garret, built to be a dry depository for firewood and the
like, was dim and dark. Such a scanty portion of light was
admitted, that it was difficult, on first coming in, to see anything. Yet, with his back toward the door, and his face
toward the window, a white-haired man sat on a low bench,
stooping forward and very busy, making shoes.

When he spoke the faintness of the voice was pitiable and dreadful. It was not the faintness of physical weakness, though confinement and hard fare no doubt had their part in it. Its deplorable peculiarity was, that it was the faintness of solitude and disuse. It was like the last feeble echo of a sound made long and long ago.

The half-opened door was opened a little farther and secured at that angle for the time. A broad ray of light fell into the garret, and showed the workman, with an unfinished shoe upon his lap, pausing in his labor. His few common tools and various scraps of leather were at his feet on his bench. He had a white beard, raggedly cut, but not very long, a hollow face, and exceedingly bright eyes. The hollowness and thinness of his face would have caused them to look large, under his yet dark eyebrows and his confused white hair, though they had been really otherwise; but they were naturally large, and looked unnaturally so. His yellow rags of shirt lay open at the throat, and showed his body to be withered and worn. He, and his old canvas frock, and his loose stockings, and all his poor tatters of clothes, had, in a long seclusion from direct light and air, faded down to such a dull uniformity of parchment yellow, that it would have been hard to say which was which.

He had put up a hand between his eyes and the light, and the very bones of it seemed transparent. So he sat, with a steadfastly vacant gaze, pausing in his work. He never looked at the figure before him, without first looking down on this side of himself, then on that, as if he had lost the habit of associating place with sound; he never spoke, without first wandering in this manner, and forgetting to speak.

Now that he had no work to hold, he laid the knuckles of the right hand in the hollow of the left, and then the knuckles of the left hand in the hollow of the right, and then passed a hand across his bearded chin, and so on, in regular changes, without a moment's intermission. The task of recalling him from the vacancy into which he always sank when he had spoken, was like recalling some very weak person from a swoon, or endeavoring, in the hope of some disclosure, to stay the spirit of a fast-dying man.

A study of these, or of any well-constructed paragraphs, will show that paragraphs, like whole compositions, must have not only well-selected details, but also *completeness, unity,* and *plan.*

The planning of paragraphs we shall study later (Chapter VIII); but that a paragraph should be complete, and that it should be a unit, are points already clear, because *each paragraph has its own subject or topic.* The outline above given states the five topics in the last selection. If, in this selection, the writer had, in the second paragraph, which treats of the old man's voice, described in part his clothing, this paragraph would have lacked the unity it now has. Every sentence in that paragraph relates to the voice which is being described. Or if, in the next paragraph, any important or striking detail, necessary to a clear and vivid picture of the old man's appearance, had been omitted, that paragraph would have lacked completeness. *Unity* and *completeness*, in compositions and in paragraphs, seem perhaps very simple and plain matters to be spoken of so much, but careless and uninstructed writers so often fail to think of these qualities and to secure them, that their importance must be insisted upon frequently.

A carefully written piece of composition may always be *outlined*, paragraph by paragraph, much as the selection just given was outlined; and all school compositions should be so outlined before being written. The pupil by thus working out his plan or order of topics secures himself against omission of important points, and against wandering from his topics while writing (secures for his composition completeness and unity). He will then write his composition with the outline before him, and his *paragraphing will follow the topical outline*. Whenever a writer finishes what he has to say on one topic of the outline, he should begin a new paragraph for the next topic, and mark the beginning by indention.

Thoughtless or ignorant writers, forgetting that each paragraph must have unity, often *indent incorrectly*. In the following selections, as printed here, the indentions are irregular and misleading.

The Battle of the Blue Licks. (From *The Choir Invisible*, by James Lane Allen, p. 67. Copyright, 1897, by The Macmillan Company.)

Let the creek here be the Licking River. The Kentuckians, some on foot and some on horse, but all tired and disordered and hurrying along, had just reached the bank. Over on the other side — some distance back — the Indians were hiding in the woods and waiting. No one knew exactly where they were; every one knew they counted from seven hundred to a thousand. The Kentuckians were a hundred and eighty-two.

There was Boone with the famous Boonsborough men, the very name of whom was a terror; there was Trigg with men just as good from Harrodsburg; there was Todd, as good as either, with men from Lexington. More than a fourth of the whole were commissioned officers, and more fearless men never faced an enemy. There was but one among them whose courage had ever been doubted, and do you know what that man did? After the Kentuckians had crossed the river to attack, been overpowered, forced back to the river again, and were being shot down or cut down in the river like helpless cattle, that man — his name was Benjamin Netherland — did this: He was finely mounted. He had quickly recrossed the river and had before him the open buffalo trace leading back home. About twenty other men had crossed as quickly as he and were urging their horses toward this road.

But Netherland, having reached the other bank, wheeled his horse's head toward the front of the battle, shouted and rallied the others, and sitting there in full view and easy reach of the Indian army across the narrow river, poured his volley into the foremost of the pursuers, who were cutting down the Kentuckians in the river. He covered their retreat.

He saved their lives. Yet when some twenty of the officers had come out before the ranks to hold a council of war, and the wisest and the oldest were urging caution or delay, one of them — McGary — suddenly waved his hand in the air, spurred his horse into the river, and shouted, "Let all who are not cowards follow me!"

They all followed; and then followed also the shame of defeat, the awful massacre, the sorrow that lasts among us still, and the loss to Kentucky of many a gallant young life that had helped to shape her destiny in the nation.

(From *The Man who Was*, by Rudyard Kipling.)

The great beam-roofed mess room of the White Hussars was a sight to be remembered.

All the mess plate was on the long table,— the same table that had served up the bodies of five dead officers in a forgotten fight long and long ago,— the dingy, battered standards faced the door of entrance, clumps of winter roses lay between the silver candlesticks, the portraits of eminent officers looked down on their successors from between the heads of sambhur, nilghai, maikhor, and, pride of all the mess, two grinning snow leopards that had cost Basset-Holmer four months' leave that he might have spent in England instead of on the road to Thibet, and the daily risk of his life on ledge, snow slide, and glassy grass slope. The servants, in spotless white muslin and the crest of their regiments on the brow of their turbans, waited behind their masters, who were clad in the scarlet and gold of the White Hussars and the cream and silver of the Lushkar Light Horse.

Dirkovitch's dull green uniform was the only dark spot at the board, but his big onyx eyes made up for it.

Exercise 17. Indention. — *Write the words that should be indented in the above selections, and be able to give reasons for the indentions as you think they should be.*

Exercise 18. Paragraph topics. — *Write the topics of the paragraphs in the above selections, after the indention has been corrected.*

There is usually in a paragraph one sentence which states or suggests the topic of that paragraph. This is called the *topic sentence.* It usually appears at or near the beginning of the paragraph, but sometimes at the end. The purpose of the topic sentence is to tell clearly and simply what is the subject of the paragraph. Thus it shows the unity of the paragraph either by *preparing* the reader for what is to be said, or by *summing up* what has been said.

In the following paragraphs the *topics* are printed as titles, or headings, and the *topic sentences* are printed in italics.

A Room and its Occupant. (From *Bleak House,* by Charles Dickens, Ch. X.)

The character of the room

The air of the room is almost bad enough to have extinguished the candle. *It is a small room, nearly black with soot, and grease, and dirt.* In the rusty skeleton of a grate, pinched at the middle as if Poverty had gripped it, a red coke fire burns low. In the corner, by the chimney, stand a deal table and a broken desk; a wilderness marked with a rain of ink. In another corner a ragged old portmanteau, on one of the two chairs, serves for cabinet or wardrobe: no larger one is needed, for it collapses like the cheeks of a starved man. The floor is bare; except that one old mat, trodden to shreds of rope yarn, lies perishing upon the hearth. No curtain veils the darkness of the night, but the discolored shutters are drawn together; and through the two gaunt holes pierced in them, famine might be staring in — the Banshee of the man upon the bed.

The occupant of the room

For, on a low bed opposite the fire, a confusion of dirty patchwork, lean-ribbed ticking, and coarse sacking, *the visitor*, hesitating just within the doorway, *sees a man.* He lies there, dressed in a shirt and trousers, with bare feet. He has a yellow look in the spectral darkness of a candle that has guttered down, until the whole length of its wick (still burning) had doubled over and left a tower of winding sheet above it. His hair was ragged, mingling with his whiskers and his beard — the latter, ragged too, and grown like the scum and mist around him, in neglect. Foul and filthy as the room is, foul and filthy as the air is, it is not easy to perceive what fumes those are which most oppress the senses in it; but through the general sickliness and faintness, and the odor of stale tobacco, there comes into the visitor's mouth the bitter, vapid taste of opium.

Burns in Edinburgh. (From *Familiar Studies of Men and Books*, by Robert Louis Stevenson, p. 77.)

He was now, it must be remembered, twenty-seven years of age; he had fought since his childhood an obstinate battle against poor soil, bad seed, and inclement seasons, wading deep in Ayrshire mosses, guiding the plow in the furrow, wielding "the thresher's weary flingin' tree"; and his education, his diet, and his pleasures had been those of a Scotch countryman. *Now he stepped forth suddenly among the polite and learned.* We can see him as he then was, in his boots and buckskins, his blue coat and waistcoat striped with buff and blue, like a farmer in his Sunday best; the heavy plowman's figure firmly planted on its burly legs; his face full of sense and shrewdness, and with a somewhat melancholy air of thought, and his large dark eye "literally glowing" as he spoke. "I never saw such another eye in a human head," says Walter Scott, "though I have seen the most distinguished men of my time."

Exercise 19. **Topics and topic sentences.** — *Bring to class, in writing, a statement of the "topics" in the following paragraphs, also the "topic sentences" copied out.*

(From *Dr. Jekyll and Mr. Hyde*, by Robert Louis Stevenson, p. 8.)

It chanced on one of these rambles that their way led them down a by-street in the busy quarter of London. The street was small and what is called quiet, but it drove a thriving trade on the week days. The inhabitants were all doing well, it seemed, and all emulously hoping to do better still, and laying out the surplus of their gains in coquetry; so that the shop fronts stood along the thoroughfare with an air of invitation, like rows of smiling saleswomen. Even on Sunday, when it veiled its more florid charms and lay comparatively empty of passage, the street shone out in contrast to its dingy neighborhood, like a fire in a forest; and with its freshly painted shutters, well-polished brasses, and general cleanliness and gayety of note, instantly caught and pleased the eye of the passenger.

Two doors from one corner, on the left hand going east, the line was broken by the entry of a court; and just at that point a certain sinister block of building thrust forward its gable on the street. It was two stories high; showed no window, nothing but a door on the lower story and a blind forehead of discolored wall on the upper, and bore in every feature the marks of prolonged and sordid negligence. The door, which was equipped with neither bell nor knocker, was blistered and distained. Tramps slouched into the recess, and struck matches on the panels; children kept shop upon the steps; the school-boy had tried his knife on the moldings; and for close on a generation no one had appeared to drive away these random visitors or to repair their ravages.

(Hamlin Garland, in the *Ladies' Home Journal*, August, 1899. By permission.)

Koweechee was a most wonderful mountain. It sprang from the lowlands of dark green hills, covered with pines as with a robe, and it reached to a dazzling dome of snow two miles above the valley where the Angry River roared. Every line was noble, sweeping, regal, and the summit burned under the noon sunlight with unearthly radiance, and glowed and lightened till it seemed as if the sky and snow were one. As the sun sank to the west, Koweechee amplified and glorified like some mighty orator stepping before a countless multitude of men. He loomed over the tall pines and intervening hills with inex-pressible grandeur—it would seem that nothing more remained of majesty to express — and when the sun went down and the stars came out behind his awful crown, then the lone traveler, crouching close beside his camp fire, lifted his eyes timidly and whispered, "Lord, I adore!"

(From *Dr. Jekyll and Mr. Hyde*, by Robert Louis Stevenson, p. 27.)

It was by this about nine in the morning, and the first fog of the season. A great chocolate-colored pall lowered over heaven, but the wind was continually changing and routing these em-battled vapors; so that as the cab crawled from street to street Mr. Utterson beheld a marvelous number of degrees and hues of twilight; for here it would be dark, like the black end of evening; and there would be a glow of rich, lurid brown, like the light of some strange conflagration; and here, for a moment, the fog would be quite broken up, and a haggard shaft of daylight would glance in between the swirling wreaths. The dismal quarter of Soho seen under these changing glimpses, with its muddy ways, and slatternly passengers, and its lamps, which had never been extinguished or had been kindled afresh to combat this reinvasion of darkness, seemed like a district of some city in a nightmare.

(From *The Sketch Book*, by Washington Irving.)

Suddenly the notes of the deep-laboring organ burst upon the ear, falling with doubled and redoubled intensity, and rolling, as it were, huge billows of sound. How well do their volume and grandeur accord with this mighty building! With what pomp do they swell through its vast vaults, and breathe their awful harmony through these caves of death, and make the silent sepulcher vocal! And now they rise in triumph and acclamation, heaving higher and higher their accordant notes, and piling sound on sound. And now they pause, and the soft voices of the choir break out into sweet gushes of melody; they soar aloft, and warble along the roof, and seem to play about these lofty vaults like the pure airs of heaven. Again the pealing organ heaves its thrilling thunders, compressing air into music, and rolling it forth upon the soul. What long-drawn cadences! What solemn, sweeping concords! It grows more and more dense and powerful — it fills the vast pile and seems to jar the very walls — the ear is stunned — the senses are overwhelmed. And now it is winding up in full jubilee — it is rising from earth to heaven — the very soul seems rapt away and floated upward on this swelling tide of harmony!

Exercise 20. Topics and topic sentences. — *Write out the topics and topic sentences of such others of the paragraphs printed elsewhere as the teacher may select.*

Note to teachers. — When completed, the following exercises, as well as many of the others, might be placed upon the blackboard, read, and criticised during the recitation period.

Exercise 21.   Arrangement of sentences in paragraphs.

EXAMPLE OF SENTENCES MISARRANGED : —

The two halves of a huge white mustache encircled his mouth, like two parentheses. This man had on his head a piece of a cocked hat, without a cockade; his dilapidated face had a stony tint, that yellow tint which old monuments have in the sunlight. He was dressed in an old uniform. They saw in front of a vineyard gate a sort of soldier. Across one of the sleeves stretched an old and worn strip of gold lace.

THE SAME SENTENCES PROPERLY ARRANGED : —

Topic — Description of an old soldier

They saw in front of a vineyard gate a sort of soldier. This man had on his head a piece of a cocked hat, without a cockade; his dilapidated face had a stony tint, that yellow tint which old monuments have in the sunlight. The two halves of a huge white mustache encircled his mouth, like two parentheses. He was dressed in an old uniform. Across one of the sleeves stretched an old and worn strip of gold lace.

Study the following paragraphs of misarranged sentences, discover the topic of each paragraph and write it as a heading; then rewrite the sentences, arranged so as to connect smoothly and naturally.

(*a*) He had a very large nose, slightly brass-colored: his cheeks were very round and very red. His doublet was prolonged behind into something like what is now termed a "swallow tail," but was much obscured by the swelling folds of an enormous black, glossy-looking cloak. It was the most extraordinary looking little gentleman Gluck had ever seen. His mustaches curled twice round like a corkscrew on each side of his mouth, and his hair, of a curious mixed pepper-and-salt color, descended far over his shoulders. He was about four feet six in height, and wore a conical pointed cap of nearly the same altitude, decorated with a black feather some three feet long.

(b) They thought their thick mats would defend them from a rifle ball as well as from a stone. Observing the flashes of the guns, they naturally concluded that water would counteract their effect. It was generally observed that at first the Indians showed great resolution in facing our firearms; but it was entirely owing to ignorance of their effect. Being soon convinced of their error, yet still at a loss to understand how so many among them were killed, they had recourse to the following plan. But finding this last resource to fail them, they soon dispersed, and left the beach entirely clear. They therefore, very sagaciously, dipped their mats or armor in the sea, just before coming on to face our soldiers.

(c) Beneath the pulpit sat the deacons, and just before them were the deaf seats and benches for the old and feeble who owned no pews. In the left-hand gallery were the young men and boys. There, too, sat the tithingman. A narrow aisle crossed the broad one midway and joined the doors on either side. The young women filled the wall pews of the right-hand gallery. The main door opened on a broad aisle that led to the high pulpit, with its green cushions and its funnel-shaped sounding board. In the front gallery sat the singers. Spinsters and elderly women were given the front row of seats. Close to the four walls was a row of pews separated by a continuous aisle from the body of the church. The little girls had benches.

Exercise 22. Paragraph making. — *Complete the paragraphs suggested by the following topic sentences:* —

(a) To-day I saw an old woman selling newspapers . . .

(b) This old high-walled garden was a very interesting and delightful place. . . .

(*c*) The tramp's most notable peculiarity was his voice. . . .

(*d*) In one of my recent walks I came upon the handsome new building of . . .

(*e*) The house has a very interesting attic, now used as a storeroom . . .

(*f*) To-day I saw a striking experiment performed in . . .

(*g*) The old mill is well worth a visit . . .

Note.—This exercise may be employed for oral or for written composition or for both, as the teacher may direct.

Exercise 23. Paragraph writing.—*Write from each of the following suggestions a paragraph. Introduce a topic sentence in each case.*

(*a*) *Our school yard.* Shape, size — position of building in it — parts of the yard — objects, trees, etc., in the yard — signs it bears of its use — scenes it has witnessed.

(*b*) *The public square* (or, a square or little park). Situation, shape, size — plan or parts — objects in it — special features.

(*c*) *A horseless carriage.* First impression — difference in appearance from other vehicles — number of seats — where its mechanism is — the steering gear, etc. — the brake — appearance when at full speed.

(*d*) *A domestic animal.* Size — limbs — proportions — coat — movements.

(*e*) *Our church.* Parts and plan — material, colors — striking features.

(*f*) *A balloon.* Twenty feet high when filled — made of silk — brown — hanging basket (for passengers) — ropes form network over balloon — ropes hold up the basket.

(*g*) *The cotton plant.* Two or three feet high — white flowers, which fall off — seed pod ripens, opens of itself — cotton plucked with seeds in it — seeds must be removed by a machine.

(*h*) *The whale.* Great size (sometimes sixty feet or more in length) — enormous mouth — tail flat, strong and heavy enough

to break a small boat — blubber or fat beneath skin — in top
of head, nostril through which the whale "spouts."

(*i*) "*The Dewey Arch.*" Erected at time of welcome to
Admiral Dewey — made of white staff, coated over a wooden
framework — as high as a four-story building — two wagons
may pass abreast through the arch — smaller side arches —
sculpture groups on faces and top.

Exercise 24. Original description. — *After reading again
Scott's description of the mansion of Tully-Veolan (p. 33)
outline and then write a complete description of some
interesting building, paying special attention to paragraphing and to the use of topic sentences. See that the
several paragraphs are smoothly connected.*

Exercise 25. Description from picture. — *Make an outline for a description of the Capitol (p. 52). Write the
topic sentences for all the paragraphs you would write
from this outline. Then write the description.*

THE CAPITOL AT WASHINGTON

CHAPTER IV

WE have seen that each part or division of a composition (each paragraph) has its own part to perform in the setting forth of the whole subject, and that it is the business of a paragraph to tell only what belongs to it. But it is important to bear in mind that each sentence, as well as each of the paragraphs and the whole composition, should have oneness or unity. For a sentence is the expression of a thought; its one business is to express that thought, no more, no less. So a sentence is not even a correct one, unless it has this quality of *unity*. Every sentence, no matter how long it is, no matter how many modifying or subordinate ideas it has, no matter how many coördinate verbs it has, can and must have unity. For so long as the less important or subordinate ideas are kept in their place, being used merely as modifiers, the sentence still has the unity that belongs to its principal idea or statement. And as for compound sentences, which state two or more ideas of equal rank or importance, such sentences also have properly a unity, because the parts or clauses must be closely connected in thought, or they are simply parts of the same thought. If not, the sentence lacks unity, and is a bad sentence.

To see how several coördinate statements may have unity, take the sentence: " We shouted until we were hoarse, and Tom hoisted a pole with a handkerchief tied to it; my brother fired his revolver, and all of us waved our arms wildly — but we could not attract their attention." Here the unity among the statements is in the idea of what was done to attract the desired attention.

To secure unity in sentences is extremely important, yet not always easy. Careless and uninstructed writers and speakers are continually uttering sentences that fail of unity. Nothing shows the poor writer more than this. In fact, the greatest lesson we can learn about good sentence making is to give every one of our sentences unity. There is one sound rule to follow: *Have for each sentence one main thought, and one only; express it, and then put the period.* If at first all your sentences are short and simple, no matter. Have no ambition to write long sentences, until you are sure you can write them as clear units.

There are three or four very common causes of failure in sentence unity.

I. *The "and" habit.*

Careless writers and speakers seem almost to think there is no other conjunction in the English language than " and." They string out idea after idea, using " and" to pin the statements together, until chance or weariness suggests coming to a stop. This is one of the commonest and one of the very worst faults in sentence making. It shows thoughtlessness and slovenliness. In every sentence there should be a principal thought or statement, and details that are subordinate in importance should be expressed as grammatically subordinate. *Note the following faulty sentences :* —

1. There is a bird on that branch, and its nest is near by, and there are three eggs in the nest.

2. Mr. Beecham came to town the other day and bought his boy a bicycle and ordered it sent out to his farm, and it was not sent for a week and Mr. Beecham was very angry about it.

3. He was getting old, and he had to be out on the wharf a good deal, and it wasn't convenient to be locking up his office, and he sent down to Machias for a school-teacher who was a sort of poor relation of his.

4. And so John saw his native village again, and it was a calm sunny day, and they descended into the green valley where the town lay, and knocked at Mr. Ericsson's door, but the house was empty.

5. In many places the forest had been cut away, and this left open tracts, and here the sweet mountain grass grew thick and strong, and there were also harebells, foxgloves, and wild pinks.

6. Hans was walking backward and forward on the mountain side, and his eyes were fixed on the ground and he did not see me approach.

7. It was in summer and the flowers were all in blossom, and he was walking along after his sheep, and all at once he saw a wonderful sky-blue flower, and he had never seen one of the kind before in all his life.

Exercise· 26.   Correction of abuse of "and." — *In each of the above sentences, select what you regard as the principal ideas, then cut each sentence up into two or more sentences having "unity," expanding the one main thought when necessary, and using relative pronouns or other connectives.* (See the table of conjunctions on page 85.) *Some of the clauses made coördinate should be put as modifiers* (phrases or clauses) *if they are really subordinate in thought.*

EXAMPLE OF CORRECTION (sentence 1):   There is a bird on that branch.   Its nest, containing three eggs, is near by.   *Or,* On that branch there is a bird, whose nest is near by.   The nest has in it three tiny eggs, of a pale blue color.

II. *Needless change of subject.*

EXAMPLE: After the fire had been lighted, the boys retreated to a shed which was some twenty feet from the house of Mr. Foote, whose family was absent from home.   (This sentence employs four words as subjects: fire, boys, which, and family.)   Changed so as to reduce the number of subjects: After lighting the fire the boys retreated to a shed near the home of Mr. Foote's absent family.

1.   When my uncle reached home, the members of his family were found to have gone out to a party.

2.   Although the captain thought the fire was a serious one, it was concluded by him that prompt action might save the house.

3.   He received us very pleasantly, and we were invited by him to take seats in the shady courtyard.

4.   The climate of Khartoum is very unhealthful, and we learned that this unfortunate gentleman had long been a resident of the place, and that he was suffering greatly from fever.

5.   There were indeed some persons, but the number of them was small, by whom a kind of hobbling march on the broken

arches of the bridge was continued, but they fell through, one after another, as so long a walk had tired them.

Exercise 27. Avoiding change of subject. — *Correct the above sentences, by reducing the number of the subjects, if possible to only one, by placing some of the statements as modifiers, or by changing verbs in the passive voice to the active voice, or the reverse.* (See the example of correction given.) *Sometimes it may be well to make two sentences instead of one.*

III. *Forgetting the verb.* — One fault that is simply bad grammar, and can appear only in very careless writing, is to omit the verb. This occurs in rather long and complex sentences, which have confused the writer himself.

EXAMPLES: 1. But Fletcher, who, after he had visited the mill, thinking he had now to cover his tracks, walked some distance in the brook.

2. But when we returned to the cottage at nightfall with the horse which had been stolen, and which was now, as we approached the house, so badly frightened that he broke away and ran into the woods.

3. The long façade, consisting only of balconied windows deeply recessed, standing erect on the summit of a considerable hill, which gives a fine plunging movement to its foundations.

4. But Frank, after he had tried again and again to break open the shutter, which was nailed at three or four places, and found he could do nothing with it.

5. Looking very weak and weary, the boy, who had evidently walked a great distance, for his face was pale and his steps were slow, coming timidly up the garden walk, and rapped at the door.

Exercise 28.   Correction of sentences. — *Rewrite the above sentences so as to make them say something clearly and grammatically. If you prefer, make two sentences to take the place of any one.*

EXAMPLE: The first above given may be corrected by omitting "who."   If this is done, "walked" becomes the principal verb, with the subject "Fletcher."

IV. *Joining unconnected ideas.*

EXAMPLES: 1. Soup is good to begin a meal with, and we were all hungry as could be.

2. Goldsmith, who had the smallpox in his youth, became a great writer before he was forty.

3. He came back on the night boat, looking much better after his two weeks' vacation.

4. He had the air of a nobleman; at the time I saw him he had on a white waistcoat.

5. When the body was pulled into the boat it was found to be clothed in the same blue suit Martin had recently bought, but all efforts to restore life were in vain.

6. I next saw the town from the stern thwart of a little sailing vessel; behind the settlement was a great gash in the hillside where granite was quarried.

7. The name of the building was The Mentone, and it was completely destroyed by the fire.

Exercise 29.   Sentence-unity. — *Correct or expand the above sentences so as to secure unity; or write reasons for thinking them faulty.*

EXAMPLE (1 above):   When one is tired and cold, a bowl of soup is the best thing to begin a meal with.   As for us, we were so hungry that anything would have tasted good.   *Or* (make a connection between the two statements given):   We were so hungry that the soup, poor as it was, seemed a delicious and satisfying thing to begin the meal with.

Exercise 30. Criticism. — *Look over one of your own compositions, sentence by sentence, to make sure that each sentence has " unity " and contains no misuse of " and." Bring to class, copied out, the incorrect sentences, and opposite them write correct or improved ones, thus: —*

The incorrect sentences. The same corrected or improved.

CHAPTER V

In Chapter II we learned that all compositions should show skillful selection and have completeness, unity, and a well-thought-out plan. Descriptions, therefore, should be full enough of well-chosen details to be satisfactory, that is, there should be no omission or oversight of important parts of the subject; and descriptions should be free from sentences or paragraphs that have no close or useful connection with the subject. As for the requirement of plan, we saw that in good descriptions the writer usually begins with a *glance* at the subject of the description, mentioning that which first or most prominently strikes the attention in it; and then that he uses the larger part or body of the description to set forth the *details* in full, arranged in some definite order, and grouped under certain divisions or heads.

In this chapter we are to consider a few ways of improving our descriptions, and we shall continue also our study of paragraphing.

I. *Point of view.* — In beginning a description, it is usually necessary, for the sake of clearness, to select a point from which to view the object or scene.

If your subject is a house, and your point of view is outside of it, you are not expected to describe any of the interior, except, perhaps, what you see from that outside position. Neither should you describe all the sides of the house, for all are not to be seen from one point of view. Sometimes, however, the observer may change his point of view during the description. He may, for instance, walk entirely round the house. Whenever the point of view is movable, the reader should be distinctly told so. Whether it is well to have a moving point of view, depends upon the nature of the subject. Of course, in describing the interior of a house of several rooms, the point of view must change from room to room. (See Dickens's description of Bleak House, quoted in Chapter II.) This is really a case, however, of several descriptions in one.

A very important result of having a certain point of view is that the *scale* of the description depends upon the *distance* of the point of view. If a writer is describing a mountain as seen from a distance of several miles, of course he will see none of the details that engage the attention of a person climbing the same mountain. The latter would write of the rocks, the fallen trunks, the brushwood, the flowers, the dead leaves, and perhaps the occasional outlook from the slopes over the broad valleys. The distant observer would see the great outlines of the mountain, the play of light and shade, the overhanging clouds.

All that can be said is, that a writer should decide carefully upon his point of view, just as a painter must select the place for his stool and canvas. Not to have clearly in mind a point of view, whether close or distant, oblique from the object or directly in front, above or below it, outside of it or inside, makes danger of vagueness and inaccuracy in the description.

Exercise 31. Points of view. — *What are the points of view in Irving's description of an inn kitchen, page 21, Mr. Kipling's description of Holden's house, page 22, Stevenson's description of Mr. Hyde, page 28, Miss Repplier's description of a street pageant, page 30, Dickens's description of the shoemaker, page 38, of a room and its occupant, page 43, Mr. Garland's description of Mount Koweechee, page 46, Stevenson's description of a London fog, page 46?*

Exercise 32. Points of view. — *(a) What were the points of view in three of the descriptions you have written? (b) What point of view would you adopt in writing a description of your room at home; of a house on fire; of a florist's window; of a snowstorm; of a race?*

II. *Use of comparison.* — Sometimes in describing a complex or extensive subject or scene, it is very useful to compare it to something simple and familiar, for this helps our readers to understand all that we say. Thus in describing the battlefield of Waterloo, Victor Hugo asks his readers to imagine a great **A**. Then he goes on to explain that the lines are roads, and that the three-cornered space is occupied by a certain hill, and so on. This comparison of the place with an A makes the entire description much clearer and simpler than it might have been. In the same way Mr. Creasy, the author of *The Fifteen Decisive Battles of the World*, makes clear his description of the battlefield of Marathon by comparing it to a crescent (the shape of the young moon). Sir Walter Scott, in describing the hall of Cedric the Saxon (in *Ivanhoe*, Ch. III), explains the arrangement of the tables by saying they formed a large T; the cross part, on a slightly raised platform, being the table at which sat Cedric and his immediate family.

The world is full of similarities, and if a writer chooses a comparison that will really explain and make distinct the thing or scene he is describing he will add much to his description. It will usually be wise for the writer of a description to pause and ask himself: "What is this like? What can I compare my subject to?"

Note the comparisons in the following description of an army hospital:

(From *The Wound Dresser*, by Walt Whitman, p. 35. By permission.)

As a specimen of almost any one of these hospitals, fancy to yourself a space of three to twenty acres of ground, on which are grouped ten or twelve very large wooden barracks, with, perhaps, a dozen or twenty, and sometimes more than that number, of small buildings, capable all together of accommodating from five hundred to a thousand or fifteen hundred persons. Sometimes these large wooden barracks, or wards, each of them, perhaps, from a hundred to a hundred and fifty feet long, are arranged in a straight row, evenly fronting the street; others are planned so as to form an immense V; and others again arranged around a hollow square. They make all together a huge cluster.

III. *Statement of effects.* — One of the strongest ways of describing anything is by telling its effect upon yourself or upon others. Instead of trying to describe the beauty of Helen, Homer tells us of the admiration and wonder the sight of her caused in the old men at the gate of Troy. So, in the description of Mr. Hyde, quoted in Chapter II of this book, the author makes us realize how horrible was the man's appearance by telling how the very sight of his deformity made the observer feel.

Always try, in describing anything, to make your reader feel as you do. Bring yourself into your descriptions, not so much, perhaps, by telling as by suggesting what you think and feel in the presence of your subject, and thus causing your reader to have those thoughts and feelings too. This gives life to what you write. If you are telling about a wretched abandoned old house, your thoughts and feelings would not be the same as if you were in a great sunny field filled with flowers. Make the reader share your own impressions. In this way you make the description distinctly your own. Do not put down just bare cold facts, but write with love of your subject, write feelingly and personally, so that if anybody reads what you write he may think and feel as you did.

IV. *Giving of sense-impressions.* — One particular form of giving your own feelings is to mention or indicate how the subject impresses your five senses. Of course, in most descriptions we are obliged to speak principally of sight-impressions; but very often there are odors and sounds to be mentioned and described, and occasionally there are impressions of touch and taste. It is extremely important to suggest sense-impressions, for, the more you mention, the more vivid and complete is the reader's idea of the thing or scene described.

First let us think how many different impressions we get only or chiefly through sight. When we look at an object we see : —

1. Its size,
2. Its shape and parts and position,
3. Its apparent texture or character,
4. Its movements, if any,
5. Its colors, and effects of light and shadow.

All these are valuable parts of the description of any visible object or scene. The details regarding *colors* may be particularly delightful, and should always be given.

Add to the five sight-impressions these others : —

6. Impressions of one's own bodily motions,
7. Of sounds,
8. Of touch, of pressure and weight, and of temperature,
9. Of odors,
10. Of taste,

and we have a wide range of impressions, whether
agreeable or disagreeable, which it is the describer's
business to convey or suggest, and which, when well
communicated, impart to a description a large element
of its merit and of its pleasure-giving qualities.

Exercise 33.   Sense-impressions. — *In the following descriptions, note (in writing) the sorts of impressions conveyed by the words or phrases in italics:* —

Description of a Landscape in France.   (From *Travels with a
    Donkey*, by Robert Louis Stevenson, p. 48.)

Pradelles stands on a hillside, *high* above the Allier, surrounded by *rich* meadows.   They were cutting aftermath on all
sides, which gave the neighborhood, this *gusty* autumn morning,
an untimely *smell of hay*.   On the opposite bank of the Allier
the land kept *mounting* for miles to the horizon ; a *tanned* and
sallow autumn landscape, with *black* blots of fir wood and *white*
roads *wandering* through the hills.   Over all this the clouds
shed a uniform and *purplish shadow* . . . throwing into
still higher relief the *twisted* ribbons of the highway.   It was a
cheerless prospect, but one *stimulating* to a traveler.

Description of Amy Falconer.   (From *The Choir Invisible*,
    by James Lane Allen, p. 3.   Copyright, 1897, by The
    Macmillan Company.)

Her *pink* calico dress, newly *starched* and ironed, had looked
so pretty to her when she had started from home, that she had
not been able to bear the thought of wearing over it this *lovely*
afternoon her *faded, much-stained* riding-skirt; and it was so
short that it showed, resting against the saddle-skirt, her *little*
feet loosely fitted into new *bronze* morocco shoes.   On her
hands she had drawn *white* half-hand mittens *of home-knit;* and
on her head she wore an *enormous white scoop* bonnet, lined
with *pink*, and tied under her chin in a *huge white muslin* bow.

Her face, hidden away under the pink-and-white *shadow*, showed such tints of *pearl and rose* that it seemed carved from the inner surface of a seashell. Her eyes were *gray, almond-shaped*, rather *wide apart*, with an expression changeful and playful, but withal rather shrewd and hard; her *light brown* hair, as *fine* as unspun silk, was parted over her brow and drawn simply back behind her ears; and the lips of her little mouth *curved* against each other, fresh, *velvetlike*, smiling.

On she rode down the avenue of the primeval woods; and Nature seemed arranged to salute her as some imperial presence; with the *waving* of a *hundred green* boughs above and on each side; with a hundred floating *odors;* with the *flash* and *rush* of *bright* wings; with the *swift* play of *nimble* forms up and down the boles of trees; and all the *sweet* confusion of innumerable *melodies*.

Willowby Heath. (From *Green Pastures and Piccadilly*, by William Black, Ch. II.)

This was Willowby Heath — a vast *stretch* of sandy ground covered by *dark* heather mostly, but showing here and there *brilliant* masses of gorse and broom, and here and there a *small* larch tree not over four feet in height, but *gleaming* with a glimmer of *green* over the dark common. A couple of miles away, on a *knoll*, stood a *windmill*, its great arms *motionless*. Beyond that again the heath darkened as it *rose* to the *horizon*, and ended in a *black* line of firs.

Exercise 34. Comparisons in descriptions. — *What comparisons are stated or suggested in the three descriptions just quoted? Write out a list, containing at least five.*

Exercise 35. Description from picture. — *(a) Make an outline for a description of the scene represented in the picture on page 68. (b) Write the description, conveying a sense of reality, as far as you can, by suggesting comparisons and sense-impressions.*

HAYMAKING

68

Exercise 36. Sense-impressions. — *Note, in a table or list, the words in the following descriptions that mention or suggest sense-impressions, and opposite each word write the sort of sense-impression conveyed.*

A Youthful Pioneer. (From *The Choir Invisible*, by James Lane Allen, p. 14. Copyright, 1897, by The Macmillan Company.)

One among them, larger and handsomer than the others, had pleased his fancy by donning more nearly the Indian dress. His breechclout was of dappled fawn skin; his long thigh-boots of thin deerhide were open at the hips, leaving exposed the clear whiteness of his flesh; below the knees they were ornamented by a scarlet fringe tipped with the hoofs of fawns and the spurs of wild turkey; and in his cap he wore the intertwined wings of the hawk and the scarlet tanager.

A Scene in Southern California. (From *A Summer in a Cañon*, by Kate Douglas Wiggin, p. 20. Houghton, Mifflin, and Company, by permission.)

The town is yet asleep, and in truth it is never apt to be fairly wide awake. The air is soft and balmy; the lovely Pacific, a quivering, sparkling sheet of blue and gray and green flecked with white foam, stretches far out until it is lost in the rosy sky; and the mountains, all purple and pink and faint crimson and gray, stand like sentinels along the shore. The scent of the roses, violets, and mignonette mingled with the cloying fragrance of the datura is heavy in the still air. The bending, willowy pepper trees show myriad bunches of yellow blossoms, crimson seed berries, and fresh green leaves, whose surface, not rain-washed for months, is as full of color as ever. The palm trees rise without a branch, tall, slender, and graceful, from the warmly generous earth, and spread at last, as if tired of their straightness, into beautiful crowns of fans, which sway toward each other with every breath of air. Innumerable butterflies and humming birds, in the hot, dazzling sunshine of

noonday, will be hovering over the beds of sweet purple helio-
trope and finding their way into the hearts of the passion
flowers, but as yet not the faintest whir of wings can be heard.
Looking eastward or westward, you see either brown foothills,
or, a little later on, emerald slopes whose vines hang heavy
with the half-ripened grapes.

The Circus Girl.   (From *Day Dreams*, by Kenneth Gra-
    hame, p. 105.)

I found myself seated actually in the circus at last, and took
in the first sniff of that intoxicating circus smell that will stay
by me while this clay endures.   The place was beset by a hum
and a glitter and a mist; suspense brooded large o'er the
blank, mysterious arena.   Strung up to the highest pitch of
expectation, we knew not from what quarter, in what divine
shape, the first surprise would come.

A thud of unseen hoofs first set us a-quiver; then a crash of
cymbals, a jangle of bells, a hoarse applauding roar, and
Coralie was in the midst of us, whirling past 'twixt earth and
sky, now erect, flushed, radiant, now crouched to the flowing
mane; swung and tossed and molded by the maddening
dance music of the band.   The mighty whip of the count in
the frock coat marked time with pistol shots; his war cry,
whooping clear above the music, fired the blood with a passion
for splendid deeds, as Coralie, laughing, exultant, crashed
through the paper hoops.   We gripped the red cloth in front
of us, and our souls sped round and round with Coralie, leaping
with her, prone with her, swung by mane or tail with her.
It was not only the ravishment of her delirious feats, nor her
cream-colored horse of fairy breed, long-tailed, roe-footed, an
enchanted prince surely, if ever there was one!   It was her
more than mortal beauty that held us spellbound.   What
princess had arms so dazzlingly white, or went delicately
clothed in such pink and spangles?

But summers sicken, flowers fail and die, all beauty but
rides round the ring and out at the portal; even so Coralie

passed in her turn, poised sideways, panting, on her steed; lightly swayed as a tulip bloom, bowing on this side and on that as she disappeared.

Near Whales at Night. (From *Two Years Before the Mast,* by R. H. Dana, Jr., p. 30.)

It was on the night that we passed between the Falkland Islands and Staten Land. We had the watch from twelve to four, and, coming upon deck, found the little brig lying perfectly still, inclosed in a thick fog, and the sea as smooth as though oil had been poured upon it; yet now and then a long, low swell rolling under its surface, slightly lifting the vessel, but without breaking the glassy smoothness of the water. We were surrounded far and near by shoals of sluggish whales and grampuses, which the fog prevented our seeing, rising slowly to the surface, or perhaps lying out at length, heaving out those lazy, deep, and long-drawn breathings which give such an impression of supineness and strength. Some of the watch were asleep, and the others were quiet, so that there was nothing to break the illusion, and I stood leaning over the bulwarks, listening to the slow breathings of the mighty creatures, — now one breaking the water just alongside, whose black body I almost fancied that I could see through the fog; and again another, which I could just hear in the distance, — until the low and regular swell seemed like the heaving of the ocean's mighty bosom to the sound of its own heavy and long-drawn respirations.

A Drive in Missouri. (From *Green Pastures and Piccadilly,* by William Black, Ch. XLIV.)

That drive up the bed of the Missouri we shall not soon forget. There was no made road at all, but only a worn track through the dense vegetation of this swampy plain, while ever and anon this track was barred across by ravines of rich, deep, black, succulent mud. It was no unusual thing for us to see first one horse and then its companion almost disappear into a hole, we looking down on them; then there would be a fierce struggle, a plunge on our part, and then we were looking up at the horses, pawing the bank above us. How the springs held out we could not understand. But occasionally, to avoid these ruts, we made long detours through the adjacent prairie land lying over the bluffs; and certainly this was much pleasanter. We went through a wilderness of flowers, and the scent of the trampled Mayweed filled all the air around us. . . . The sunflowers were higher than our animals' heads; they could not possibly see where they were going; but, all the same, they slowly ploughed their way through the forest of crackling stems. . . . The air was thick with insect life, and vast clouds of reedbirds rose, as we passed, from the sunflowers. There was a red fire all over the west as we finally drove into the valley of the Decatur.

Rubens's Painting, Samson and Delilah. (From George Eliot's Letters, in her Life, by J. W. Cross.)

[I was] delighted afresh in the picture of "Samson and Delilah," both for the painting and the character of the figures. Delilah, a magnificent blonde, seated in a chair, with a transparent white garment slightly covering her body, and a rich red piece of drapery round her legs, leans forward, with one hand resting on her thigh, the other, holding the cunning shears, resting on the chair — a posture which shows to perfection the full, round, living arms. She turns her head around to look with sly triumph at Samson — a tawny giant, his legs caught in the red drapery, shorn of his long locks, furious with the consciousness that the Philistines are upon him, and that this time he cannot shake them off. Above the group of malicious faces and grappling arms a hand holds a flaming torch. Behind Delilah, and grasping her arm, leans forward an old woman, with hard features full of exultation.

Exercise 37. Imitation of model. — (a) *Write, in imitation of one of the descriptions given in Exercises 33 and*

*36, a description of some place in the country that you
remember very well, or of some scene in a park, or of a
garden.* (b) *Give orally an imitation of another of the
descriptions given in the same exercises.*

Exercise 38. Topics and topic sentences. — *Write the
topics and the topic sentences of the paragraphs quoted
in Exercises 33 and 36.*

Exercise 39. Outlining of paragraphs. — *Outline any
three of the paragraphs in Exercise 36.*

Exercise 40. Paragraphs from summaries. — (a) *From
the following suggestions write descriptive paragraphs,
introducing sense-impressions.* (See descriptions of similar subjects quoted previously.) (b) *Reproduce orally one
of your own descriptions.*

(a) *The Pasha's son.* Age about eleven — tall for his age
(form) — face, eyes (colors) — smile (impression made) — he
made a graceful salutation, just as (comparison) — voice (impression made) — manners.

(b) *The home of a Russian serf.* Supper ready (odors) —
in one corner a picture of Mary and Jesus, the figures covered
with gilt (color) — except the hands — these blackened by smoke
of a tiny lamp (colors) — fire burning (light and shadows) —
boiled potatoes steaming in a big wooden bowl — salt, plate of
melted fat, loaf of black bread — no plates, knives, or forks —
rough wooden spoons (form) — all ate from the bowl (movement; comparison) — for drink, a thin and rather sour beer
(taste; invent a comparison).

(c) *The bay on a windy day.* The water (color), furrowed
(comparison) — the water flecked with foam (color, comparison)
— bare, empty of vessels — all the sails now huddled at the
wharves, like (comparison) — the wind from off the water (effect
on sense of feeling; odor).

(d) *At night among the pines.* I wakened thirsty — drank
a tin of cold water (feeling and effect) — stars clear (colors,

comparison) — Milky Way (color, form) — all around me the firpoints (color) stood upright and stock still — my donkey munching at the grass the only sound except that of the brook (describe this sound) — the colors in the sky.

Exercise 41. Original description. — (*a*) *Prepare an outline for a complete original description of a landscape, a street scene, a picture, an audience, or a classroom.*

(*b*) *Write the description, introducing all the direct sense-impressions you can.*

CHAPTER VI ·

WHILE it is of the first importance in our writing that we shall have something to say, and shall know how to arrange and present our paragraphs and their contents, we should at no time lose sight of the great need all writers have for skill in the formation of sentences. In this chapter are to be studied the parts or elements of sentences, the kinds of sentences, and some of the transformations of which sentences are capable. Now we must, through the patient practice afforded by many exercises, acquire skill in thus changing and manipulating sentences. Only in this way may we be able to make and select the sentence-form that is best suited to each case. Necessarily a good deal of what follows is in the nature of a review and application of English grammar.

I. *Kinds of elements.* — In the study of grammar [1] we learn that a *sentence* consists of two principal parts, the *subject* (the word or words denoting that about which something is said), and the *predicate* (expressing what is said of the thing denoted by the subject). The subject may *be* a word, a phrase, or a clause; and it may be *modified* by a word, a phrase,

---

[1] See Maxwell's *Advanced Lessons in English Grammar*, Ch. V, p. 39.

or a clause. The verb in the predicate may also be modified by one or more words, phrases, or clauses. (Remember that a *clause* always has in it a subject and a predicate.)

A noun (or a noun expression), whether it be a subject, an object, a predicate noun (sometimes called attribute), or the noun part of a prepositional phrase, may be modified by an *adjective* element. (For example, the word " element " in the last sentence belongs with the preposition " by," and is modified by "an" and "adjective.") A verb may be modified by one or more *adverbial* elements, and, if transitive, may have one or more *object* elements. So we may form this *table of elements:* —

I. *Principal elements*

    a. Subject

        1. Word (a noun or a pronoun)

        2. Phrase (usually an infinitive verb)

        3. Clause

    b. Predicate, always a verb, with or without complements or modifiers

II. *Subordinate elements*

    a. Predicate complement or attribute (of intransitive verb)

        1. Word

        2. Phrase (an infinitive verb, or else a preposition with its object)

        3. Clause

b. Object complement (object of transitive verb)

    1. Word

    2. Phrase (usually an infinitive verb)

    3. Clause

c. Adjective element

    1. Word (including adjectives, nouns in apposition, nouns or pronouns in the possessive case)

    2. Phrase (either an infinitive verb, or a preposition with its object)

    3. Clause (always introduced by a relative pronoun, or by a word like *where, wherein,* etc., used as the equivalent of a preposition and a relative pronoun)

d. Adverbial element

    1. Word

    2. Phrase (infinitive or prepositional)

    3. Clause (introduced by one of the subordinating conjunctions; see page 85)

Exercise 42. Kinds of elements. — *In the above table there are five groups, each group containing three subdivisions. There are, therefore, fifteen forms of elements to be known (not including the verb, which is found in all sentences). Write, in order, fifteen sentences, illustrating the fifteen forms of elements enumerated in the table. Underline in each sentence the element you intend as the example.*

Exercise 43. Transformation of elements. — *In the following sentences change the italicized words to phrases, and the italicized phrases to words. In each case, after* *making the transformation, tell what kind of element you have made, and tell what it modifies (unless it is a principal element,—a subject).*

EXAMPLES: (*a*) That maple tree *with the golden leaves* may be seen *from a great distance.*

CHANGED: That *golden-leaved* maple tree may be seen *afar.*

(*b*) *Seeing* is *believing.*

To see is *to believe.*

(*c*) He is a man *of stern severity.*

He is a *stern* and *severe* man.

1. The laws *of nature* are just.   2. Windsor Castle has long been a residence *of kings and queens.*   3. He has done his work *with thoroughness.*   4. "Happiness" is a *stronger* word than "felicity."   5. The offer is certainly *to be accepted.*   6. Writing *about a man's life* is not an easy form of literature.   7. *Playing* quoits is a game *of small merit.*   8. His object was *to secure* that money.   9. It is *of no use to send* him away.   10. What is *of more bitterness* than *seeing* one's children ungrateful?

II. *Kinds of sentences.* — We further learn in the study of grammar that sentences are *simple, compound,* or *complex.* A simple sentence is a sentence containing one subject and one predicate (but either the subject or the predicate, or both, may be composed of two or more parts of equal importance, as, two noun subjects or two verbs; there is then said to be a " compound subject " or a " compound predicate "). A simple sentence may be lengthened by the addition of modifiers; but so long as these modifiers are *words* or *phrases,* and not *clauses,* the sentences are still simple sentences.

Exercise 44.   Formation of simple sentences. — *If we take apart a simple sentence like this:—*

After a refreshing walk of about two miles we reached the corner of a high stone wall running parallel with the road,

we get separate elements like these: —

We had a refreshing walk. It was a walk of about two miles. Then we reached the corner of a wall. It was a high wall. It was of stone. It ran parallel with the road.

Each of the following groups of separate elements you are to combine into a good simple sentence. Be sure that you use in each sentence but one subject-element and one verb-element (though the subject or the predicate may be compound).

Note. — Other exercises of this sort are found in Maxwell's *Advanced Lessons in English Grammar*, p. 45.

1. He could scarcely sit still in the house. This was during the first few days. He could scarcely take part in the studies. Mr. Lorne had chosen these studies for him.

2. It was a great triumph for his mother. . It was especially a triumph for his sister. His sister was now a bright, blooming girl. She was sixteen years old.

3. He had a restless look. He had a rather unhappy look. This was very different from the bright eyes and the pleasant countenance of Otto. Otto was his best friend.

4. Old Gregor and his grandson were returning home. They were coming through the forest. They had bundles of wood. The old man was stooping low under the weight of the heavy sticks.

5. He set out in a direction opposite from home. He was armed with a club. He expected to find another bear.

A *complex sentence* is one that contains one or more dependent or subordinate clauses, but only one principal clause. Any sentence that contains two or more principal clauses (no matter how many subordinate clauses) is a *compound sentence.*

Exercise 45. Formation of easy complex sentences. — *Form complex sentences from the following sets of simple sentences, by using suitable connectives and making necessary contractions.*

EXAMPLES : (*a*) I saw a boy start up and run after his cattle. The last one of the cattle was entering the forest.

I saw a boy start up and run after his cattle, the last one of *which* was entering the forest.

(*b*) The boy was singing. I came out of the thicket.

As I came out of the thicket, the boy was singing; or,

While the boy was singing, I came out of the thicket.

Note. — Similar exercises are to be found in Maxwell's *Advanced Lessons in English Grammar*, p. 48.

1. I seated myself in the shade. I wished to enjoy the view.
2. The first object attracting my attention was Otto. He was knitting beside his herd of cows. This was his usual occupation.
3. We stepped back a few paces. We sat down on the ground. We desired to bring the box between us and the blue sky. (Purpose.)
4. Other bees come. They quarrel with the first bees. (Use a time clause.)
5. It was a hemlock tree. It stood in a niche in a wall of rocks. These were hoary and moss-covered. They were thirty feet high.

Exercise 46. Formation of compound sentences. — *Form compound sentences from the following sets of simple sentences, and tell which clauses are principal and which subordinate.*

EXAMPLE : To the southwest the soil is a tough clay. To the northeast the gardens consist of a warm crumbling mold, very fertile.

To the southwest the soil is a tough clay, while to the northeast the gardens consist of a warm crumbling mold, very fertile.

Note. — Similar exercises are to be found in Maxwell's *Advanced Lessons in English Grammar,* p. 50.

1. Our wells, at an average, run to about sixty-three feet. When sunk to that depth they seldom fail.

2. The north wind is blowing hard. It must be a cold day.

3. It was the first of May. Snow was falling.

4. His name was James. It may have been John.

5. He lay back in the steamer chair in his hall room. The shadows began to lengthen a little. The long day drew nearer to its end.

6. He roused himself. The hand organs had both gone away. The child next door had ceased her piano practicing.

7. With an effort he raised himself. He saw a line of carriages on the other side of the street. They were moving slowly toward the corner.

8. He was thinking about himself. He was thinking about his hopes. They had been as bright as the sunshine of spring. He was pondering over his bitter disappointment.

9. He saw the long shafts of level sunshine. They entered his window. He took heart again. He recalled the great things accomplished by one man.

10. The dogs were barking. Cattle bells were jangling in the wooded pastures. The youth passed farmhouses. Lights in the kitchen windows showed that the women were astir about breakfast. He heard the sounds of voices and currycombs at the barn. The men were at their daily chores.

Most compound sentences may be changed into complex sentences, and many complex sentences may be changed into compound. But these changes make some difference in the meaning, and therefore one or the other sentence in every case is the better. *Usually the complex* sentence is better than the compound, because there is *generally but one principal idea* or statement in a sentence, and the other statements should be put in the form of subordinate clauses, participial modifiers, phrases, adjectives, or adverbs. No exercises will be given in the transformation of complex sentences into compound, but the opposite transformation it is very important to understand.

Exercise 47. Transformation of compound sentences into complex. — *Put all but one of the clauses in each of the following sentences into the form of subordinate clauses, so as to make complex sentences. Be very careful to keep for the principal clause the statement which you think is the most important in the sentence.*

EXAMPLES: (*a*) He did wrong, and his father punished him.

Changed: His father punished him because he had done wrong; or, As he had done wrong, his father punished him.

(*b*) You have only twenty marbles, and I have five more than you.

Changed: If you have only twenty marbles, I have five more than you.

1. The mercury dropped suddenly, and I knew a storm was coming.

2. The horse felt the fly and shook himself at once.

3. He spoke always in a whisper, and this lent him an air of mystery.

4. I needed all the money I could save, and I came most of the way by canal boat.

5. "He'll teach him," said Mr. Lightly, and he laughed and coughed.

6. They might open these letters, and I might be kept here many years longer.

7. I promised to deliver both letters with my own hands, and the man parted from me in more cheerful spirits.

8. You sign this paper, or I sue you for the money.

9. I found the Pasha's house, but I was not admitted, because the Egyptian women are not allowed to receive the visits of strangers.

10. I bring you this letter, and I promised your father I would deliver it into your own hands.

Exercise 48. Transformation into simple sentences. — *(a) Change the above compound sentences, or the complex sentences into which you transform them, into simple sentences. Observe that an adjective or adverbial clause may in many instances be changed into a phrase or even into a word element. Since this change secures brevity and simplicity, it is often a good one to make. But the more expanded form may sometimes be easier to read and understand.*

EXAMPLES of this kind of change : —

a. The valleys which produce grass enough for the cattle are generally scattered widely apart.

Changed to a simple sentence: The valleys producing grass enough for the cattle are generally scattered widely apart.

b. In the front of the house, where the sun shone warmest, he had laid out a little garden.

In front of the house, in the place warmed most by the sun, he had laid out a little garden.

c. The farmer determined that he would not sell his corn.

The farmer determined not to sell his corn.

d. The storm did damage that could not be repaired.

The storm did irreparable damage.

(b) Change in similar ways the following to simple sentences: —

1. He was a man whose character was above reproach.

2. As nature had done so much for Athens, it is fortunate that art did so much more.

3. One day as I stood on a street corner in a great city, I saw above the trucks and the traffic a line of bees that were carrying off sweets from some grocery.

4. He leapt from bed as the sun was rising.

5. After there had been some days of impatient expectation, the king landed at Margate, which was then an important port.

6. It was a book that one could read with enjoyment.

7. When he saw the woman open the door, he dodged back again behind the fence.

8. However differently the thirteen colonies may have been founded or governed, they were all alike in some respects that were very important.

9. The tumult was such that it could not be described.

10. Others were governed by the original proprietors or by those who represented them.

11. Find single words for the following expressions: In a high degree, it is possible that, with earnestness, for that reason, a great amount of (unhappiness), through his whole life.

One of the most serious troubles writers have in making sentences is due to a failure to see what is the *principal* idea, of which the others must be *modifiers*. Nearly always when several sentences are connected by "and," one of the statements should clearly be made the principal one. The others may be subordinated to it by a proper use of conjunctions.

Learn to use complex sentences instead of compound.

Now a skillful use of complex sentences is impossible without a knowledge of the kinds and meanings of the English conjunctions.

Cónjunctions may be classified as follows: [1] —

I. *Coördinating conjunctions*

   a. Copulative or additive — and, also, moreover, likewise, both . . . and, not only . . . but also

   b. Adversative — but, yet, still, however, while, whereas, though, and yet, though . . . yet

   c. Disjunctive — or, else, or else, otherwise, either . . . or, neither . . . nor

   d. Illative or consequential — therefore, hence, so, and so, so that, consequently, then, so then, wherefore, accordingly

II. *Subordinating conjunctions*

   e. Introductory — that, whether, if

   f. Causal — because, since, as, for, inasmuch as, whereas

   g. Purposive — that, in order that, so that, lest

   h. Concessive — though, although, even if, inasmuch as, notwithstanding

   i. Conditional — if, provided, supposing that, unless

   j. Adverbial — when, how, where, as, why, whither, as if, while

   k. Comparative — than, as

[1] Compare Maxwell's *Advanced Lessons in English Grammar*, pp. 202, 203.

To these, for the present purpose, may be added a class of words that serve both as pronouns and as connectives : —

> *l.* Relative pronouns — which, who, that, as, what; whichever, whoso, etc. Certain conjunctive adverbs, as where, wherein, whereto, where-at, -on, -upon, -by, etc., are frequently used as equivalent to a preposition and a relative pronoun, and introduce adjective clauses.

The correct use of any of the subordinating conjunctions makes a *complex* sentence, while the coördinating conjunctions, when used to connect clauses, form compound sentences. (See Maxwell's *Advanced Lessons in English Grammar*, section 465.)

Exercise 49. Formation of complex and of compound sentences. — *Combine each of the following groups of simple sentences into (a) a compound sentence, (b) a complex sentence. (c) Whenever it is possible, change the resulting sentence into a simple sentence.*

Mark with a star which of the three sentences, (a), (b), or (c), you think to be the best one, and be prepared to tell why.

In making change (b) the letter placed after each group of simple sentences refers you to the table of conjunctions just given and suggests what relation between the clauses is to be expressed.

EXAMPLE : I came home at seven o'clock. My brother had already returned.

Changed (*a*) to a compound sentence: I came home at seven o'clock and my brother had already returned.

(*b*) to a complex sentence: When I came home at seven o'clock my brother had already returned (time clause used).

(*c*) to a simple sentence: By the hour of my coming home, seven o'clock, my brother had already returned.

Here, of course, the complex sentence is best, since it expresses most clearly and briefly the true relation between the two statements given to be combined. The compound sentence (*a*) is a distinctly bad sentence.

1. The piece of quartz was pure white. My father gave it to me. (*l*)

2. Marion looked at his sister. He nodded. (*j*)

3. This has been one of the warmest days of the summer. Of that there can be no doubt. (*e*)

4. The winter was now coming on. I had to complete my house very rapidly. (*f*)

5. He determined to make the visit. He had to borrow money to pay his way. (*h*)

6. Goldsmith was not well supplied with money. Johnson had no more. (*k*)

7. I stayed out under the tree a quarter of an hour longer. I knew I should get wet. (*i*)

8. They wrap the trunk and boughs in woolen cloth. The severity of the winter might kill the tree. (*g, d*)

9. They came at length to the very top of the hill. They had a fine prospect of the surrounding country. (*l*)

10. I made haste to scramble to my feet. I could see who the newcomer was. (*f, g, d*)

Skill in making the various kinds of transformations or substitutions that have now been spoken of, and skill in making and selecting the three kinds of sentences, will do something toward giving one's writing ease and variety in form of expression. A

good deal of practice in these substitutions and in
sentence formation is necessary to the making of a
good writer. The ignorant or unskillful writer writes
tiresome and monotonous sentences, mostly compound, or else very short, simple sentences. Learn
to say much in simple sentences by using modifiers ;
and learn to write complex sentences easily. Study
the table of conjunctions, and use the different kinds
as they are required, so that you will not overwork
the conjunction " and." (See pages 54–56.)

**Exercise 50. Combination of short statements into good
paragraphs.**

EXAMPLE OF SHORT SENTENCES TO BE COMBINED : —

Washington was elected general of the army. He was at
this time forty-three years of age. In stature he a little exceeded six feet. His limbs were sinewy and well proportioned.
His chest was broad. His figure was stately. It had dignity of
presence. It had ease of manner. His constitution was robust.
It had been tried and invigorated by his early life in the wilderness. It had been tried and invigorated by his habit of occupation out of doors. Also by his rigid temperance. In
consequence of these facts few equaled him in strength of
arm. Few equaled him in power of endurance. His complexion was florid. His hair was dark brown. His head was
in its shape perfectly round. . . . His eyes were dark blue.
They were deeply set. They had an expression of resignation. They had an earnestness that was almost sad.

EXAMPLE OF COMBINATION : —

(Description of the appearance of George Washington.)

When Washington was elected general of the army he was
forty-three years of age. In stature he a little exceeded six
feet; his limbs were sinewy and well proportioned; his chest

broad, his figure stately, blending dignity of presence with ease of manner. His robust constitution had been tried and invigorated by his early life in the wilderness, his habit of occupation out of doors, and his rigid temperance; so that few equaled him in strength of arm or power of endurance. His complexion was florid, his hair dark brown, his head in its shape perfectly round. . . . His dark blue eyes, which were deeply set, had an expression of resignation and earnestness that was almost sad. — GEORGE BANCROFT.

Combine the following sentences into well-written paragraphs, making the proper headings and underscoring the topic sentences: —

(*a*) I had my own little sled. It was filled with hay. It was covered with reindeer skins. These things were to keep me warm. So long as the weather was not too cold, it was very pleasant to speed along. I sped through the dark forests. I sped over the frozen rivers. Or I went past farm after farm in the sheltered valleys. I went up hill and down. I rode until long after the stars came out. It was very pleasant then to get a warm supper.

(*b*) When Sir Roger is diverting himself in the woods or the fields, I have a companion at the house. He is a venerable man. He is always at Sir Roger's. He has lived at his house over thirty years. He is Sir Roger's chaplain. This gentleman is a person of good sense. He is a man of some learning. He lives a very regular life. His conversation is obliging. He heartily loves Sir Roger. He knows he is very much in Sir Roger's esteem.

(*c*) On the other side of the high town the houses stand closer. Yet they leave the same space for a little walk. This walk is shaded by sycamores. From it one looks down on the whole southern reach of the lake. The lake opens wide to the horizon. It is edged there like the sea. But in the summer sunshine it looks like a well of blue. This well of blue looks as if it was what the sunbeams drank to make the sky of.

CHAPTER VII

NARRATION

ONE who writes an account of the real or imaginary events or happenings which a narrative contains, must have in mind two points: —

First, these events or happenings must in some way be *connected*, that is, they must all be thought of either as having chiefly to do with some one person, or as having occurred at certain places, or as relating to some one idea or plan.

Second, these events or happenings must be told in some *intended order*, which should be definitely thought out beforehand by the writer.

Both these points (unity and plan) are what we must chiefly keep in view when we study the outlining of a narrative. Let us bear in mind that outlining always means *grouping*, that is, getting the minor points in a composition arranged under *headings*. We can grasp and carry in mind a small number of headings or main topics much better than we can a large number of coördinate minor topics. In addition to the advantages of plan, unity, and completeness, this is another reason why it is helpful to make outlines. It is like putting twenty or thirty small packages into two or three baskets; in that way they are much more easily carried.

Now, how can we find headings under which to group the minor events of a narrative? Suppose there are thirty events or happenings to be told, how can they be grouped? There are three principal sorts of head topics under which the events of a story may be grouped: —

1. Periods,
2. Places,
3. Chief events.

We may divide the whole narrative into sections or *periods* of time. Thus the events of Longfellow's life may be grouped under these headings: (*a*) Period of childhood and education, 1807–1825. (*b*) Period of early travel in Europe, 1825–1829. (*c*) Period of professorship at Bowdoin, 1829–1835. (*d*) Period of professorship at Cambridge, 1835–1882. In outlining a man's life[1] by periods, do not use commonplace headings, which might be used for any man's life, such as "boyhood," "manhood," "old age." After the words " period of " put, in each case, words showing the character of the period in that particular narrative. To illustrate the method of periods from a work of fiction, the events of the story of *Evan-*

---

[1] In outlining the life of a man we may use (as one form of division by periods) the man's successive *occupations*. Thus, to illustrate from Milton's life we might use the headings: (*a*) Milton's life as schoolboy and college youth, 1608-1632. (*b*) His earlier life as poet, 1632-1641. (*c*) His life as political writer and essayist, 1641-1660. (*d*) His life as writer of epic poems, 1660-1674.

geline may be grouped under : (*a*) Period of love.
(*b*) Period of hope and search. (*c*) Period of despair.
Or, the story of *Rip Van Winkle* may be divided
into : (*a*) Period of idleness. (*b*) Period of sojourn
in the mountains. (*c*) Period of renewed life in the
village.

Exercise 51. Outlining by periods. — *Read carefully
the following summary of the life of Lincoln, then outline it, using periods for main headings :* —

Abraham Lincoln — born in Hardin County, Kentucky, 1809
— when Lincoln was eight, his father moved to Indiana —
region then a wilderness — schools very rare — boy grew up
in pioneer life — learned to read, write, and cipher — at nine-
teen Lincoln went on a flatboat to New Orleans as a hired
hand — in 1830 family moved to Macon County, Illinois —
Lincoln hired out as a hand and later as a clerk in a country
store — borrowed a grammar and other books — volunteered
in the Black Hawk Indian War — studied surveying — 1834
elected to state legislature — studied law — reëlected several
times — practiced law — married 1842 — elected one term to
Congress 1846 — made many antislavery speeches from 1854
on — 1860 nominated and elected for the presidency — directed
the movements of the war — issued Emancipation Proclama-
tion 1863 — reëlected as President — witnessed end of war —
assassinated, 1865, by Wilkes Booth.

Exercise 52. Writing from outline. — *Using your outline of the above summary, (a) tell orally, in complete
sentences, the life of Lincoln; (b) write a brief life of
Lincoln, paragraphing with care, and introducing all
the particulars given.*

In outlining by *places*, which is not always possible, we have to group merely according to the

chief scenes of the events. Thus, in outlining the life of Longfellow, we might use these headings : —

(*a*) Life in Maine. (*b*) In Europe. (*c*) At Bowdoin College. (*d*) At Cambridge, Massachusetts.

The life of Shakspere is easily outlined by places : —

(*a*) Life in Stratford, 1564–1586. (*b*) In London, 1586–1611. (*c*) Last years at Stratford, 1611–1616.

Or, in outlining Shakspere's play, *The Merchant of Venice* (see Lamb's *Tales from Shakspere* for the story, which may well be used as a reading lesson), we might group the events under : —

(*a*) In Venice (the bond given ; Jessica's elopement). (*b*) At Belmont (the three suitors and the caskets ; the news of Antonio's losses). (*c*) In the Court of Justice, Venice (Shylock punished). (*d*) Closing scenes at Belmont.

Exercise 53. Outlining a narrative by places. — *Group the minor incidents in the following story under headings that indicate places. After the outline is made, reproduce the story orally, following the outline.*

JOHN GILPIN'S RIDE

John Gilpin was a citizen of credit and renown ;
A train-band captain eke was he of famous London town.
John Gilpin's spouse said to her dear, " Though wedded we have been
These twice ten tedious years, yet we no holiday have seen.

" To-morrow is our wedding day, and we will then repair
Unto the Bell at Edmonton, all in a chaise and pair.
My sister and my sister's child, myself and children three,
Will fill the chaise ; so you must ride on horseback after we."

He soon replied, " I do admire of womankind but one,
And you are she, my dearest dear, therefore it shall be done.
I am a linen draper bold, as all the world doth know;
And my good friend the calender will lend his horse to go."

Quoth Mrs. Gilpin, " That's well said; and, for that wine is dear,
We will be furnished with our own, which is both bright and
   clear."
John Gilpin kissed his loving wife; o'erjoyed was he to find
That, though on pleasure she was bent, she had a frugal mind.

The morning came, the chaise was brought, but yet was not
   allowed
To drive up to the door, lest all should say that she was proud.
So three doors off the chaise was stayed, where they did all get
   in;
Six precious souls, and all agog to dash through thick and
   thin.

Smack went the whip, round went the wheels; were never folks
   so glad;
The stones did rattle underneath, as if Cheapside were mad.
John Gilpin at his horse's side seized fast the flowing mane,
And up he got, in haste to ride, but soon came down again.

For saddle-tree scarce reached had he, his journey to begin,
When, turning round his head, he saw three customers come in.
So down he came; for loss of time, although it grieved him sore,
Yet loss of pence, full well he knew, would trouble him much
   more.

'Twas long before the customers were suited to their mind,
When Betty, screaming, came down stairs, "The wine is left
   behind!"
" Good lack!" quoth he; "yet bring it me, my leathern belt
   likewise,
In which I bear my trusty sword when I do exercise."

Now Mrs. Gilpin (careful soul!) had two stone bottles found,
To hold the liquor that she loved, and keep it safe and sound.
Each bottle had a curling ear, through which the belt he drew,
And hung a bottle on each side, to make his balance true.

Then over all, that he might be equipped from top to toe,
His long red cloak, well brushed and neat, he manfully did
　　throw.
Now see him mounted once again upon his nimble steed,
Full slowly pacing o'er the stones with caution and good heed.

But finding soon a smoother road beneath his well-shod feet,
The snorting beast began to trot, which galled him in his seat.
So, "Fair and softly," John he cried, but John he cried in
　　vain;
The trot became a gallop soon, in spite of curb and rein.

So, stooping down, as needs he must, who cannot sit upright,
He grasped the mane with both his hands, and eke with all his
　　might.
His horse, which never in that sort had handled been before,
What thing upon his back had got did wonder more and more.

Away went Gilpin, neck or naught; away went hat and wig;
He little dreamed when he set out of running such a rig.
The wind did blow, the cloak did fly like streamer long and
　　gay,
Till, loop and button failing both, at last it flew away.

Then might all people well discern the bottles he had slung;
A bottle swinging at each side, as hath been said or sung.
The dogs did bark, the children screamed, up flew the windows
　　all,
And every soul cried out, "Well done!" as loud as he could
　　bawl.

Away went Gilpin, who but he! his fame soon spread around;
"He carries weight! He rides a race! 'Tis for a thousand
    pound!"
And still, as fast as he drew near, 'twas wonderful to view
How in a trice the turnpike men their gates wide open threw.

And now, as he went bowing down his reeking head full low,
The bottles twain, behind his back, were shattered at a blow.
Down ran the wine into the road, most piteous to be seen,
Which made his horse's flanks to smoke as they had basted
    been.

But still he seemed to carry weight, with leathern girdle braced,
For all might see the bottle necks still dangling at his waist.
Thus all through merry Islington these gambols he did play,
And till he came unto the Wash of Edmonton so gay.

And there he threw the wash about on both sides of the way,
Just like unto a trundling mop, or a wild goose at play.
At Edmonton his loving wife from the balcony spied
Her tender husband, wondering much to see how he did ride.

"Stop, stop, John Gilpin! Here's the house!" they all at once
    did cry;
"The dinner waits, and we are tired!" Said Gilpin, "So am I!"
But yet his horse was not a whit inclined to tarry there;
For why? his owner had a house, full ten miles off, at Ware.

So like an arrow swift he flew, shot by an archer strong;
So did he fly — which brings me to the middle of my song.
Away went Gilpin, out of breath, and sore against his will,
Till at his friend the calender's his horse at last stood still.

The calender, amazed to see his neighbor in such trim,
Laid down his pipe, flew to the gate, and thus accosted him:
"What news? what news? your tidings tell; tell me you
    must and shall;
Say why bareheaded you are come, or why you come at all?"

Now Gilpin had a pleasant wit, and loved a timely joke;
And thus unto the calender in merry guise he spoke:
"I came because your horse would come: and, if I well fore-
bode,
My hat and wig will soon be here, they are upon the road."

The calender, right glad to find his friend in merry pin,
Returned him not a single word, but to the house went in;
Whence straight he came with hat and wig — a wig that flowed
behind,
A hat not much the worse for wear, each comely in its kind.

He held them up, and in his turn thus showed his ready wit,—
"My head is twice as big as yours; they therefore needs must
fit.
But let me scrape the dirt away that hangs upon your face;
And stop and eat, for well you may be in a hungry case."

Said John, "It is my wedding day, and all the world would
stare
If wife should dine at Edmonton and I should dine at Ware."
So, turning to his horse he said, "I am in haste to dine:
'Twas for your pleasure you came here, you shall go back for
mine."

Ah, luckless speech and bootless boast! for which he paid full
dear;
For, while he spoke, a braying ass did sing most loud and
clear;
Whereat his horse did snort, as he had heard a lion roar,
And galloped off with all his might, as he had done before.

Away went Gilpin, and away went Gilpin's hat and wig:
He lost them sooner than the first; for why? — they were
too big.
Now Mrs. Gilpin, when she saw her husband posting down
Into the country far away, she pulled out half a crown;

And thus unto the youth she said, that drove them to the Bell,
" This shall be yours, when you bring back my husband safe
    and well."
The youth did ride, and soon did meet John coming back
    amain,
Whom in a trice he tried to stop, by catching at his rein;

But not performing what he meant, and gladly would have
    done,
The frightened steed he frightened more, and made him faster
    run.
Away went Gilpin, and away went postboy at his heels;
The postboy's horse right glad to miss the lumbering of the
    wheels.

Six gentlemen upon the road thus seeing Gilpin fly,
With postboy scampering in the rear, they raised the hue and
    cry:
"Stop thief! stop thief! a highwayman!" — not one of
    them was mute,
And all and each that passed that way did join in the pursuit.

And now the turnpike gates again flew open in short space,
The tollmen thinking as before that Gilpin rode a race.
And so he did, and won it too, for he got first to town,
Nor stopped till where he had got up he did again get down.

Now let us sing, " Long live the king," and Gilpin, long live
    he,
And when he next doth ride abroad may I be there to see.

WILLIAM COWPER.

Finally, in outlining by *chief* events, we select for
headings those few turning points in the narrative,
on which many minor events and details hinge or

depend. Thus, to outline the life of Franklin (1706–1790), we might use the headings: —

(*a*) Franklin learns printing in Boston, 1718. (*b*) He goes to Philadelphia, 1723. (*c*) Publishes the first Poor Richard's Almanac, 1732. (*d*) Goes to London as colonial representative, 1757. (*e*) Is chosen an American representative to Paris, 1776.

Or, to outline a narrative poem by chief events, we may take for illustration *Paul Revere's Ride* (see Longfellow's *Tales of a Wayside Inn*): —

I. Introduction — the subject of the tale

II. Body of the narrative

(*a*) Paul Revere arranges to be signaled from the church tower
1. Signals are agreed upon
2. Revere sets out
3. His friend learns of the intended march of the British

(*b*) The friend climbs the tower
1. Sees from there the British troops setting forth
2. Revere waits impatiently in Charlestown
3. The signal is given

(*c*) The ride begins
1. He reaches Medford
2. He passes through Lexington
3. He arouses Concord

III. Conclusion — the results of that ride

Caution must be taken, in using this last method, that each head topic is an *event* or *occurrence*. Do not fall into the error of mingling in one outline two or all of the three methods we are considering (periods, places, chief events). Keep the three entirely distinct. Decide which method you purpose using in an outline, and then keep to it strictly. Also in using any method state all your main topics in a *similar form*, whether that of brief sentences, or that of nouns with modifiers.

Exercise 54. Outlining of narrative poems. — (*a*) *Outline in a similar way at least two of the following poems either by "chief events" or by "periods"; (b) then tell or write the stories, using your outlines as guides:—*

King Robert of Sicily	H. W. Longfellow
The Skeleton in Armor	H. W. Longfellow
The Bell of Atri	H. W. Longfellow
The Ballad of Carmilhan	H. W. Longfellow
The Falcon of Ser Federigo	H. W. Longfellow
The Vision of Sir Launfal	J. R. Lowell
(For this purpose omit the preludes.)	
Hervé Riel	Robert Browning
The Pied Piper of Hamelin	Robert Browning
Maud Muller	J. G. Whittier
The Garrison of Cape Ann	J. G. Whittier
Horatius at the Bridge	T. B. Macaulay
Alice Brand	Sir Walter Scott
Lady Clare	A. Tennyson
The Passing of Arthur	A. Tennyson
Dora	A. Tennyson
Lord Ullin's Daughter	T. Campbell
Bishop Hatto	R. Southey
The Prisoner of Chillon	Lord Byron

Sir Patrick Spens . . Old ballad
Sir Hugh (Hugh of Lincoln) . Old ballad
Bewick and Grahame . . Old ballad
 (See the title Ballads, in Appendix V.)

Exercise 55. — *Outline some prose story you have read lately, by "periods" and then by "chief events," in each case putting in the minor events; then compare the two outlines and decide which is preferable for that story.*

Using your outline as a guide, reproduce, orally or in writing, the story.

Stories suitable for use in this exercise may be found in such books as the following: —

A Wonder Book . . Nath. Hawthorne
Twice-Told Tales . . Nath. Hawthorne
The Age of Fable . . Thomas Bulfinch
Tales from Shakspere . . Charles and Mary Lamb
Tales of a Traveler . . Washington Irving
Christmas Stories . . Charles Dickens
In Ole Virginia . . Thomas N. Page
Main Traveled Roads . . Hamlin Garland
Van Bibber and Other Stories Richard H. Davis

Exercise 56. Outlining a biography. — *Outline the life of some American by "places," or by "chief events," introducing the more important details of his life as subtopics.*

Construction of narratives. — When we write a narrative, there are four sorts of reasons why our readers may be interested: (*a*) The events themselves, and the order in which they are told, in other words, what we call the story or plot, may be a source of interest; (*b*) The characters of the persons in the narrative may be interesting; (*c*) The scene or scenes of the events (what may be called the background or setting of the principal figures and events) may be interesting; and (*d*) In the works of able and excellent writers, the style of the writing, that is, the language used, and the personal qualities of the writer as shown in what he says, should be no small source of interest and pleasure. To repeat, then, good narratives are enjoyed on account of : —

1. *The style :* —

The language used may be clear, smooth, and musical, equal to all demands upon it for the expression and suggestion of emotions.

The writing may contain wit, humor, sympathy, pathos, wisdom, acuteness.

2. *The scenes or setting :* —

Which may be interesting because of familiarity, or of strangeness; of beauty, or of sadness and horror.

3. *The characters,* which may be interesting because they are : —

Made to seem lifelike,

Shown as resourceful, heroic, and admirable,

Shown as contemptible, or unfortunate, or

Made comical or entertaining.

4. *The plot or story,* which may be interesting because of : —

The strangeness or extraordinariness of the events,

The element of mystery,

Our natural sympathy with characters placed in the particular situation described, in which they have difficulties to overcome and ends to accomplish, or,

The working out of some plan or idea.

As far as the plot alone is concerned, it may be said that the element of mystery is what chiefly interests us in ghost stories and in detective stories; the element of strangeness or remarkableness, in adventure stories, stories of travel, or comic stories; and the elements of natural sympathy and curiosity, in stories of difficulties overcome or of success achieved, as in stories of undertakings, or of events that work out definite consequences.

In reading a work of fiction, we should think about all four of the sources of interest given in the table above. By so doing we not only shall get much more enjoyment out of what we read, but shall become able to form intelligent opinions of books and able to give reasons for liking them or disliking them, in whole or in part.

Exercise 57. Study of interest. — *Using the above outline, think carefully over some story you are familiar with, chosen by yourself or by the teacher, and write down the reasons for its being interesting to you. (1) Under the head of style, write whether the book or story has, in your opinion, any of the qualities named in the outline. (2) State what the setting or background of the events is, and for what reasons it is interesting. (3) State which of the characters are interesting, and why. (4) State for what reasons, given in the table above, the plot is interesting.*

Exercise 58.   Study of interest. — *Write a list of five narratives or stories (in prose or verse) which you have read, and under the name of each write the reason or reasons why the plot is interesting, why one of the characters is interesting, and why the setting or scene is interesting.*

Exercise 59.   Narration from picture. — *Think out a story suggested by the picture on page 105, make an outline, and write the story, seeking to make it interesting by reason of the scenes, the characters, and the events.*

Brief narratives or anecdotes are usually interesting because of the nature of the events, or because of some point they illustrate, whether comical or serious. But even in these the interestingness of characters and of scenes should not be lost sight of.

Exercise 60.   Anecdotes. — *Bring to class two anecdotes, or interesting brief narratives, found by you in a newspaper or elsewhere. (a) Write down, referring to the outline we have been studying, the reasons for the selection's being interesting. (b) Tell the anecdotes orally.*

Exercise 61.   Anecdotes and historical sketches from summaries.

MODELS FOR STUDY

(*a*) *The Sphinx.*   (From *The Age of Fable*, by Thomas Bulfinch.)

Shortly after this event, the city of Thebes was afflicted with a monster which infested the highroad. It was called the Sphinx. It had the body of a lion, and the upper part of a woman. It lay crouched on the top of a rock, and arrested all travelers who came that way, proposing to them a riddle,

with the condition that those who could solve it should pass safe, but those who failed should be killed. Not one had yet succeeded in solving it, and all had been slain. Œdipus was not daunted by these alarming accounts, but boldly advanced to the trial. The Sphinx asked him, "What animal is that which in the morning goes on four feet, at noon on two, and in the evening upon three?" Œdipus replied, "Man, who in childhood creeps on hands and knees, in manhood walks erect, and in old age with the aid of a staff." The Sphinx was so mortified at the solving of her riddle that she cast herself down from the rock and perished.

(b) *Perry's Victory.* (From Eggleston's *History of the United States.*)

A little fleet was launched on Lake Erie in 1813, and its officers and men were anxious to rival the glory of the American ships at sea. In the battle of Lake Erie, fought this year, Commodore Perry hung up for his signal, "Don't give up the ship!" the dying words of Lawrence. When his flagship was riddled and disabled by the enemy, he got into a small boat and was rowed to another vessel, standing upright while the enemy was raining shot about him. Reaching the ship *Niagara*, he sailed down on the British line and broke it, and at length compelled the whole fleet to surrender. At the close of the battle, Perry wrote to General Harrison, "We have met the enemy, and they are ours."

Write out or tell orally the stories suggested in these summaries, seeking to interest your readers, not only by the nature of the incidents, but also by the characters of the personages, and by the description of an attractive or unusual scene or setting: —

(a) *Legend of William Tell.* The Swiss ordered to toss their caps in the air at sight of Gessler, the Austrian — Tell refuses — is arrested — is found to be renowned as a skillful archer — is made by Gessler to shoot at an apple which is placed on the head of Tell's son — the arrow pierces the apple — Tell is found to have concealed other arrows under his coat — " To kill thee, tyrant, had I slain my boy ! "

(b) *The bundle of sticks.* Quarreling brothers — father cannot make them friendly — has sons try to break bundle of sticks — both fail — then bundle is undone — the separate sticks are easily broken — quarrelsome brothers are like separated sticks — in union there is strength.

(c) *The hare and the tortoise.* The hare makes fun of the tortoise's slowness — the tortoise offers to race the hare — the tortoise starts off — the hare laughs at the idea of such an easy race — decides to take a nap — when he awakes the tortoise has reached the goal.

(d) *A retort.* Samuel Foote had a wooden leg — a person one day amused himself by remarking on this limb — Foote became annoyed — at last he said, " Why do you attack me on my weakest part? I never said anything against your head!"

(e) *The Pilgrims.* They move from England to Holland — decide to come to America — prepare to depart — ship, the *Mayflower* — the voyage —landing in December — settlement at Plymouth — hardships of the winter — why we remember the Pilgrims.

(f) *The battle of Trenton.* Fifteen hundred hired Hessian soldiers stationed at Trenton — on Christmas night, 1776, Washington crossed the Delaware — it took all night to cross — river full of floating ice — Hessians stupefied from their drinking and reveling of the night before — they were surprised at light in the morning — a thousand taken prisoners.

(g) *Discovery of gold in California.* Existence of the gold long known to the Indians and Mexicans of that region — the discovery on the Sacramento in 1848 — the rush of gold seekers in 1849 — dangers of the long journey overland or by way of the Isthmus of Panama — hard and dangerous life in California — the result.

Exercise 62.   Writing from picture. — *Write a story sug-gested by this picture.*

In writing a story of your own, if it is a true story, it is not worth telling unless the occurrences are more or less interesting.   If the characters or the places are also interesting, so much the better.   A great deal depends upon the way the story is begun.   It is usual to suggest in the first few sentences or in the first paragraph the setting of the narrative — the time, the scene, some of the characters.   You may bring your own feelings or ideas somewhat into the composition, by explanations or remarks, humorous or otherwise.   If the story is an invented one, see to it that, for some of the reasons we have been studying, it is made interesting. Let the story have a center of interest, and let the incidents lead up to the situation of greatest interest.

Exercise 63. Developing original narratives. — *Write out the following suggested narratives, or write similar brief narratives from subjects chosen by yourself. Indent carefully for the paragraphs, and mark in each paragraph the topic sentence. In writing do not forget the characters and the scenes or surroundings, as sources of interest.*

(*a*) *The story of our camping out.* How we came to think of it — who talked it over — where we decided to go — what we took — how we got to the place — the pitching of the tent — the cooking of meals — what we all did — incidents — the breaking up — the return.

(*b*) *A country boy's visit to the city.* How he came to go — getting ready — catching the train — the railway journey — what he first saw in the city — incidents — places visited — the most remarkable sight of all — the return home.

(*c*) *A picnic by the river.* The company — the preparations — the weather — how the members of the party got to the river — what the boys did during the morning — what the girls did — the dinner — the fishing — the games played — the ride homeward.

Exercise 64. Reproductions. — (*a*) *Select a poem mentioned in the list in Exercise 54, one that you have not previously reproduced, and develop it into a carefully written story. Avoid the language of the poem; merely tell the story in your own words.*

(*b*) *Select a story told in one of the books named in Exercise 55, read it once or twice very carefully, then write from memory the story, imitating the language of the original as closely as you can.*

Exercise 65. Original narration. — *The problem is to work up a true story, known to you, of an adventure. When you come to write it, you will have to describe the scene and the chief characters (not all at first), and to tell the events in an interesting way.*

(a) First, prepare a careful outline of the entire composition, using places or chief events or periods for the headings.

(b) Write the story, introducing description wherever necessary, but holding to your outline and telling the story clearly and connectedly. Attend to the paragraphing. In this the outline will guide you.

CHAPTER VIII

CLEARNESS IN WRITING

THERE is no use in writing at all unless you make clear what you have to say. It is not enough to write so that you may be understood; you ought to write so that you cannot be misunderstood. Language is for the communication of ideas. If your reader does not understand what you meant to say, there is no communication, and you may as well not have written. Therefore, whatever you write, write clearly.

Of course, no one can write clearly without thinking clearly. You must know and understand completely what you wish to say, or else it is useless for you to begin. The only way to do is to write about what you know and understand. Do not attempt subjects that are difficult, abstract, or unfamiliar. Take simple, easy, and above all near-at-hand topics at first, topics about which you can write of your own knowledge; and in writing upon these do not try to utter ideas or to talk about supposed facts that you do not comprehend. For instance, avoid all such subjects as The Ideal, Fortune, Virtue and Happiness, Miserliness, Generosity; better write about an insect, or a plant, or an old chair, or something you saw or did last week or yesterday, things upon which you can direct your five senses and actually learn and know something, than try to write on an object you have never seen or an idea nobody can ever see, a place you have never visited or a feeling you never experienced. Stuff written about vague, lofty, or far-off themes is usually lacking both in clearness and in interest. But when you have written from your own knowledge or experience, no matter how common and simple the subject, your writing is far more likely to be not only intelligible but readable.

But aside from understanding precisely what you want to say, there are some difficulties met with in the use of language itself; and to learn to avoid certain faults in sentence making will do much to secure clearness in all that you write.

I. *Lack of unity.*— In the first place, having unity in all your sentences will do a great deal toward making them clear. We have studied unity in Chapter IV, so we need say no more about it here than to notice that when two or more ideas, unconnected in thought, are put together in one sentence, the effect is confusing, and the sentence fails to express any idea with sufficient clearness. Or, when a number of ideas, connected in thought, but some of them important and some unimportant, are strung along in one sentence full of " ands," the sentence is pretty certain to lack clearness, simply because it does not emphasize the really important idea, but offers a jumble of several ideas, most of which should be merely modifiers.

For examples of sentences thus lacking in unity and clearness, see those referred to in Exercise 26.

II. *Omitting necessary words.*—To omit words that are necessary to the sense is a much commoner fault than may be supposed.

(*a*) Sometimes it is merely a matter of good grammar, as in such sentences as the following (further illustrations are given in Exercise 28, and in Exercise 129):—

1. Such mistakes always have and always will happen.
(Good English requires the word "happened" after "have.")
2. He knows better than go there.
3. Look up in the dictionary every word the spelling of which you are not certain.
4. She is as old, if not older, than her brother.
5. I have for over a year, and I will still continue, to pay my rent promptly.
6. I do not think he is any taller, if as tall, as I am.
7. You are the man whom the letter is addressed.

(*b*) Sometimes such words as *other, else,* or *before* are carelessly omitted. Examples:—

1. This has been a greater exposition than was ever attempted.
(The word "before" must be inserted after "ever"; otherwise the statement is untrue.)
2. Nobody ever knew so much about fishes as Agassiz did.
3. No period of ten years ever saw so much progress in science as the last ten years have seen.
4. She thinks nobody knows so much as she does.
5. I believe no one ever saw so beautiful a sunset as this.
6. I think no dog ever had so fine a coat as this one has.
7. New York is larger than any city in this country.

(*c*) Sometimes a necessary verb, preposition, or other part of speech is omitted in statements of comparisons, after *than* or *as*.   Examples: —

1. He likes me more than you.
(Insert " he does " after " than," or " do " after " you," according to which is meant.)
2. Marmosets are as much like men as some monkeys.
3. That dog looks more like a wolf than a bloodhound.
4. This meat belongs to this dog rather than that.
5. He wished for it more than his brother.
6. He wished for nothing more than a dog.
7. That stone resembles a dumpling more than anything else.

(*d*) Examples of other faulty omissions, including the omission of the *article* : —

1. If dead, his wife and children may apply.
2. This blacksmith can repair the machine when injured.
3. The wise and (the) good are all too few.   (What difference is made by the inserting of " the " ?[1])
4. We know how likely the loss of all was, when we think how thick the fog was, and especially we remember how the wind blew.
5. Some persons cannot tell the difference between the use of a colon and ∧ a semicolon.
6. The society elected a secretary and ∧ treasurer, who were to hold office for one year.
7. I believed ∧ the man was honest and ∧ he was accused falsely.
8. He selected out of the herd all the white and ∧ black horses.
9. I cannot remember ∧ one thing he said.
10. If he is not a scoundrel, he is very near ∧ one.

[1] See Maxwell's *Advanced Lessons in English Grammar*, p. 133.

11. For that crop of grass, though ∧ green and fresh, the farmer got only five dollars a ton.

12. $5000 reward if you can set fire to anything after washing in flamine.

Exercise 66. Supplying faulty omissions.—*Correct all the sentences given in the four groups given above as illustrating faulty omissions.*

III. *Faulty use of pronouns.*—One of the commonest faults of thoughtless writers is the use of a pronoun without a perfectly certain antecedent. Pronouns in themselves mean nothing; they merely stand for their antecedents. Hence it is foolish to put into a sentence a pronoun of whose antecedent the reader may not be certain.

EXAMPLES: (*a*) Mary asked her mother how old she was.

Mary said to her mother, "How old are you?" (Or, "How old am I?")

(*b*) On the mountain, at one place, there was a stone face, which we had much trouble in reaching.

On the mountain, at a place which we had much trouble in reaching, there was a stone face.

Exercise 67. Obscure pronouns. — *Correct the following sentences, either by using direct quotation, by changing the arrangement of the words, or by making clear in some other way what is the antecedent of each pronoun that is doubtful in meaning.*[1]

1. He made that remark without leaving me a chance to make a reply, which I thought was very wrong.

2. The gentleman told his brother that the umbrella he had borrowed was worthless, and so he returned it.

[1] See Maxwell's *Advanced Lessons in English Grammar*, pp. 246-247.

3. Henry called yesterday to see my father, for he had written to him to make the engagement to do so.

4. There are many pets of different characters, which are all good enough.

5. He says there is near here one dangerous place, and that is certainly worth knowing.

6. When the Indians stole his horses, he said they were worthless beasts that ought to be shot.

7. Among the new arrivals was Mr. Derby, now so loved by every one, who was to officiate on the occasion.

8. He said he had talked with the agent, and he would do all he could to prevent the injustice.　This is just what I wanted.

9. The poor boy said his father used to beat him till he was out of breath.

10. He was surprised, he said, that he had not done as he was directed to do.

11. On the opposite sides of the bridge are walks for foot passengers that are about three feet wide.

12. He was a man of great height, and that accounted for his being able to see.

13. They issued a circular concerning the horse thief, that offered a reward of ten dollars for his arrest.

IV. *The "which" habit.* — Sometimes a sentence is made very uncertain in meaning and very tiresome by the careless repeating of "which," "who" or "that" with different antecedents. A familiar example is the tale in which we read, "This is the dog that worried the cat that caught the rat that ate the malt that lay in the house that Jack built." It is needless to say that sentences like this are amusingly lacking in unity; yet we sometimes find examples like those below, written in all seriousness. One relative in a sentence is usually enough, unless the relatives refer to the *same antecedent* and the clauses are connected by coördinating conjunctions.

EXAMPLE: These words, *which* were not meant as a joke, seemed funny to the audience, *which* had not expected a speech to be so serious, *which* Mark Twain delivered.

CORRECTED: Though these words were not meant as a joke, they seemed funny to an audience which had not expected a speech of Mark Twain's to be so serious.

Exercise 68. The " which " habit. — *Rewrite the following sentences so as to give them clearness and unity. One good device is to write in place of a relative clause an adjective modifier, either a word or a phrase, or a noun in apposition.*

1. Burnes, whose father was a business man who had accumulated a tolerable fortune, grew up in idleness, which was very much to his taste.

2. The suit of clothes, which was much the worse for the wear and tear which it had received in the summer which its owner had spent in the mountains, had still to be of service.

3. The point in which he most excelled was the use of the tomahawk, which he could hurl with a skill which amazed us.

4. This story winds at first like a quiet brook, which leads here and there across green fields, which gradually give way to a stern and rocky region in which there are abrupt cataracts.

5. He had no books excepting an old copy of *Paradise Lost*, which he read in the intervals of his work, in which way he acquired some of the knowledge of good poetry which gave him pleasure all through his life.

V. *Misplacing of modifiers.*— Words, phrases, and clause modifiers may all be misplaced, and frequently are. In fact, this misplacing is *the most common of all the faults of sentence making.* It is sometimes called "squinting construction." When a modifier squints, or can be taken as belonging to one or the other of two words in the sentence, the statement may, of course, be taken in two ways, and is therefore not clear. One of the most frequently misplaced words is "*only*." Be sure to place it where it can limit only what you intend it to limit.[1]

Note the different meanings of the following sentences : —

> Only I saw three men.
> I saw only three men.
> I saw three men only.
> I only saw three men.

Another class of words often misplaced is *participles*. As a rule, when a sentence begins with a participle, the latter is understood to modify the subject of the sentence, as in the following examples : —

> Trusting to hear from you soon, I remain your friend, E. S. S.
> Brought to a halt in that direction, the animal faced about toward us.

It is very important also to remember this caution, that when two words are used correlatively (as *both . . . and, not only . . . but (also), either . . . or,* etc.), each member of the pair should come before the same part of speech. Thus in the sentence " John not only had to walk the whole distance, but to carry his little brother a part of the way," *not*

[1] See Maxwell's *Advanced Lessons in English Grammar*, pp. 260–263.

only should come after *had*, so that the correlatives may stand next to the coördinate infinitives.

Exercise 69. Misplaced modifiers. — *Correct the following sentences, by rearrangement or by substitution of equivalent expressions for the modifiers, so as to make the sentences mean clearly one thing and one thing only.*

EXAMPLE: For rent, a well-furnished parlor, for a lady, thirty-five feet wide.

CORRECTED: For rent, a well-furnished parlor, thirty-five feet wide, suitable for a lady.

1. For that crop of grass, though it was green and fresh, the farmer only got five dollars a ton.
2. Tell him, if he thinks so, he should stay at home.
3. Thinking this amusing, like a fool, he never suspected treachery.
4. I was almost allowed to do as I pleased.
5. That talk is only fit for the dullest of company.
6. He only receives four dollars a week, and has nearly spent all of it before the week is half gone.
7. He had only been there two days.
8. Rising upon tiptoe, the mere top of the gable could be seen from where he stood.
9. This rug was bought by a firm in Troy, costing over a hundred dollars.
10. Having removed the top of the jar, the mysterious contents were displayed to our sight.
11. Crowned by a tuft of poplar trees, we at last saw the hill that rose near our destination.
12. Trusting to hear from you favorably, believe me sincerely yours.
13. The train had already rounded the curve, carrying over a hundred passengers, when the engineer saw the danger signal, and, reversing the lever, the train stopped.

14. A dog that had long belonged to a man living during those years in Cairo, never having been ill a day, suddenly died.

15. I never remember to have heard a more convincing argument.

16. He not only looked at rugs but at carpets.

17. This is neither the time for idleness nor for play.

18. The teacher said we should not aim merely to memorize the lesson, but to understand it.

19. It is a country not more attractive to the farmer than to the soldier.

20. He spoke both like a manly fellow and a kindly one.

21. He did not wish to be president but still to remain in the position to which he was accustomed.

Exercise 70. Lack of clearness. — *Examine one of your recently written compositions for examples of the misplacing of modifiers, the improper use of pronouns, faulty omissions of words, or for other causes of lack of clearness. On a sheet of paper write, opposite all your sentences lacking clearness, corrected or improved sentences of the same meaning.*

Exercise 71. Composition. — *(a) Prepare an outline for a description of a street scene that you have witnessed.*

(b) Write the composition, mentioning impressions of colors, shadows, movement, form, odors, etc. (See page 65.)

(c) After writing, look the composition over and correct all sentences lacking, for any reason, in clearness.

(d) Copy the corrected composition into the exercise book.

CHAPTER IX

SINCE all we say goes into our paragraphs, it is extremely important that we learn what to put into these developments of the topics on hand. Given a topic, what shall we say about it? What ways are there of treating it? We have already seen that since each well-made paragraph has its distinct topic, or deals with its own particular part of the whole composition, everything in the paragraph must have to do with this topic, otherwise there would be a lack of unity. Now for the question, how may we fill out, illustrate, or develop the topic, so as to make our handling of it interesting and adequate?

First, a caution: no matter what we say in a paragraph, our sentences should be *connected* in thought; they should follow one another easily and naturally throughout each paragraph. This is one reason why topic sentences are useful. When we read a topic sentence, we naturally expect the explanation of it, and thus the paragraph reads *smoothly*. An emphatic word in one sentence suggests the beginning of the next remark, and thus we go on without effort from sentence to sentence.

What shall be written in paragraphs?— There are several ways of developing paragraphs, and with all these ways we should be familiar. Which of them we should use in a given case depends, as we shall see, upon the kind of composition, the nature of the topic, and what we desire to say.

I. *Details or particulars.* — If the topic is a *single* object, scene, pe·son, incident, or the like, the paragraph consists usually of details or particulars. For example, in the following paragraphs (descriptive), the topic is in one case an English farm, in the other a country church. In such a case the subject is a single scene, and the natural way to deal with it is to give particulars about it.

On one of these solitary houses, the afternoon sun, about to descend before very long behind the hills, was still lingering on this May afternoon we are describing, bringing the whitewashed porch and the broad bands of white edging the windows, into relief against the gray stone of the main fabric, the gray roof overhanging it, and the group of sycamores and Scotch firs which protected it from the cold east and north. The western light struck full on a copper beech which made a welcome patch of warm color in front of a long gray line of outhouses standing level with the house, and touched the heckberry blossom which marked the upward course of the little lane connecting the old farm with the road; above it rose the green fell, broken here and there by jutting crags, and below it the ground sank rapidly through a piece of young hazel plantation, at this present moment a sheet of bluebells, toward the level of the river. There was a dainty and yet sober brightness about the whole picture.

— From *Robert Elsmere*, by Mrs. Humphry Ward, Ch. I.

I am fond of loitering about country churches; and this was so delightfully situated, that it frequently attracted me.

It stood on a knoll, around which a small stream made a beautiful bend, and then wound its way through a long reach of meadow scenery. The church was surrounded by yew trees, which seemed almost coeval with itself. Its tall Gothic spire shot up lightly from among them, with rooks and crows generally wheeling about it.

—From *The Sketch Book*, by Washington Irving.

The following paragraph shows how the method of particulars and details is used in narration : —

The history relates that Sancho Panza was conducted from the court of justice to a sumptuous palace, where, in a great hall, he found a magnificent entertainment prepared. He no sooner entered than his ears were saluted by the sound of instruments, and four pages served him with water to wash his hands. The music having ceased, Sancho now sat down to dinner in a chair of state, placed at the upper end of the table; for there was but one seat, and only one plate and napkin. A personage, who, as it afterward appeared, was a physician, took his stand at one side of his chair, with a whalebone rod in his hand. They then removed the beautiful white cloth, which covered a variety of fruits and other eatables. Grace was said by one in a student's dress, and a laced bib was placed, by a page, under Sancho's chin. Another, who performed the office of taster, now set a plate of fruit before him, but he had scarcely tasted it when, on being touched by the wand bearer, it was snatched away, and another containing meat supplied its place. Yet before Sancho could make a beginning, it vanished, like the former, on a signal of the wand. Sancho was surprised at this proceeding, and looking around him, asked if this dinner was only to show off their sleight of hand. "My lord," said the wand bearer, "your lordship's food must here be watched with the same care as is customary with the governors of other islands. It is my duty to see that the governor eats what is good and salutary, and

prevent his touching whatever I imagine may be prejudicial to
his health. It was for that reason, my lord," continued he,
"I ordered the dish of fruit to be taken away, as being too
watery, and that other dish as being too hot, and overseasoned
with spices, which are apt to provoke thirst."

—From *Don Quixote*, by Cervantes.

The following anecdote of a walk with Sir Walter
Scott, containing both description and narration, is
an illustration of the use of the method of particulars
in writing that intermingles these two kinds of
composition :—

Everything that was beautiful and picturesque caught his
attention in an instant. I remember walking out with him
and a lady, who was staying in the house at the time, along
the sunny banks of the Tweed, toward Selkirk. It was a
bright morning, and two great and very beautiful staghounds
accompanied us in the ramble. Sir Walter pointed out the
beauties of the scene with great animation, stumping along the
little narrow path we were following, supported by a stout
stick. He had a plain Scotch bonnet on his head, and a gray
shepherd's maade or plaid round his broad shoulders, and,
when not excited, he looked, with his somewhat heavy
features, and white, overhanging eyebrows, like a good, stout,
portly farmer. About half a mile from Abbotsford, however,
a bright, sparkling stream crossed the path on its way toward
the Tweed, forming a little still pool by the side of the road
before it took another leap down the bank; and by the side of
this pool one of the staghounds, which had run on before,
stopped for some moments to contemplate his own image in the
mirror, throwing himself into the most graceful attitude
imaginable. The dog's proceeding immediately caught the
attention of the poet, and he turned to point it out to our fair
companion with his face all sparkling with eager admiration.
The gray eye lighted up, the heavy mouth beamed with a

bright smile, and even the stalwart figure became more erect and stately. " Look at the vanity of the creature," he cried, " did ever lady before her looking-glass show more admiration of herself than that brute ? "

— From The Bride of Landeck, by G. P. R. James, p. 48.

II. *Instances or examples.* — The second method of developing a paragraph is used when the topic is not a single object, but a *general topic or statement,* such as, Women are sometimes very brave, No person is faultless, " Time is money," The recent increase in the cost of living. Topics like these are naturally explained or developed by giving instances or examples of what is being discussed. This method may be used in description as in the following paragraph. The topic is indicated in the first sentence ; the other sentences give selected instances of the fog's being everywhere : —

Fog everywhere. Fog up the river, where it flows among green aits and meadows; fog down the river, where it rolls defiled among the tiers of shipping, and the waterside pollutions of a great (and dirty) city. Fog in the Essex marshes, fog on the Kentish heights. Fog creeping into the cabooses of collier-brigs; fog lying out on the yards and hovering in the rigging of great ships; fog drooping on the gunwales of barges and small boats. Fog in the eyes and throats of ancient Greenwich pensioners, wheezing by the firesides of their wards; fog in the stem and bowl of the afternoon pipe of the wrathful skipper, down in his close cabin; fog cruelly pinching the toes and fingers of his shivering little 'prentice boy on deck. Chance people on the bridges peeping over the parapets into the nether sky of fog, with fog all round them, as if they were up in a balloon, and hanging in the misty clouds.

— From Bleak House, by Charles Dickens, Ch. I.

The method of instances or examples is occasionally used in narration; very frequently in explanatory paragraphs (exposition); and a good deal used in argument, because instances of the truth of a proposition are proofs of it. Sometimes a paragraph is made up of merely one important instance or example.

Further illustrations : —

At last I fell into some talk, at a distance, with this poor man. First I asked him how people did thereabouts. "Alas, sir," says he, "almost desolate; all dead or sick. Here are very few families in this part or in that village" — pointing at Poplar — "where half of them are dead already, and the rest sick." Then he pointed to one house: "There they are all dead," said he, "and the house stands open; nobody dares go into it. A poor thief," says he, "ventured to steal something, but he paid dear for his theft, for he was carried to the church-yard too, last night." Then he pointed to several other houses, "There," says he, "they are shut up; you see a watchman at the door; and so of other houses."

— From *A Journal of the Great Plague*, by Daniel Defoe.

In some respects the animals excel us. The birds have a longer sight, besides the advantage by their wings of a higher observatory. A cow can bid her calf, by secret signal, prob-ably of the eye, to run away, or to lie down and hide itself. The jockeys say of certain horses, that "they look over the whole ground."

— From R. W. Emerson, Essay on Manners.

His children, too, were as ragged and wild as if they belonged to nobody. His son Rip, an urchin begotten in his own likeness, promised to inherit the habits, with the old clothes, of his father. He was generally seen trooping like a colt at his mother's heels, equipped in a pair of his father's cast-off galligaskins, which he had much ado to hold up with one hand, as a fine lady does her train in bad weather.

— From *Rip Van Winkle*, by Washington Irving.

The structure of every organic being is related, in the most essential, but often hidden manner, to that of all the other organic beings with which it comes into competition for food or residence, or from which it has to escape, or on which it preys. This is obvious in the structure of the teeth and talons of the tiger; and in that of the legs and claws of the parasite which clings to the hair on the tiger's body. But in the beautifully plumed seed of the dandelion, and in the flattened and fringed legs of the water beetle, the relation seems at first confined to the elements of air and water. Yet the advantage of plumed seeds, no doubt, stands in the closest relation to the land being already thickly clothed with other plants; so that the seeds may be widely distributed and fall on unoccupied ground. In the water beetle, the structure of its legs, so well adapted for diving, allows it to compete with other aquatic insects, to hunt for its own prey, and to escape serving as prey to other animals.

—From *The Origin of Species*, by Charles Darwin.

Exercise 72. Study of paragraphs. — *Write out (a) the topic of each of the paragraphs so far quoted in this chapter, and (b) the first and the last words of the topic sentences.*

(c) Mention what things are given as "instances" or "examples."

(d) Write also the kind of composition found in each of the extracts (see Chapter I).

Exercise 73. Writing of paragraphs. — *Develop the following topics or topic sentences by giving instances or examples: —*

1. Many interesting games may be played in the sand.
2. America has already produced some excellent poets.

3. Sometimes ludicrous mistakes are made through ignorance or carelessness.

4. Swimming birds.

5. Boys' sports are not always without danger.

6. The best fruits grow in the temperate zone.

7. Damages caused by bad roads and rough streets.

III. *Comparisons or contrasts.* — A third method of working up a topic is by the use of comparisons or contrasts; that is, by explaining the resemblance of the topic to something else, or by showing how it is different from something else. In each case particulars and details are given, but they are particulars about the resemblance or the contrast. In the following paragraph the two parts of the valley which is being described are made more distinct to our minds by contrast.

During the greater part of its course the valley of Long Whindale is tame and featureless. The hills at the lower part are low and rounded, and the sheep and cattle pasture over slopes unbroken either by wood or rock. The fields are bare and close-shaven by the flocks which feed on them; the walls run either perpendicularly up the fells or horizontally along them, so that, save for the wooded course of the tumbling river and the bush-grown hedges of the road, the whole valley looks like a green map divided by regular lines of grayish black. But as the walker penetrates further, beyond a certain bend which the stream makes halfway from the head of the dale, the hills grow steeper, the breadth between them contracts, the inclosure lines are broken and deflected by rocks and patches of plantation, and the few farms stand more boldly and conspicuously forward, each on its spur of land, looking up to or away from the great masses of frowning crag which close in the head of the valley, and which from the moment they come into sight give it dignity and a wild beauty.

— From *Robert Elsmere*, by Mrs. Humphry Ward, Ch. I.

In the following paragraph the idea of character is made more distinct by contrasting it with another idea : —

There is a difference between character and reputation. Character is what a man is; reputation is what he is thought to be. Men of good character are generally men of good reputation, but this is not always the case, as the motives and actions of the best of men are sometimes misunderstood and misrepresented. But it is important, above everything else, that we be right and do right, whether our motives and actions are properly understood and appreciated or not.

— Edmund Burke.

One form or variety of the method of contrasts is the telling of what a thing is not, or what it is not like. For example : —

The scene around was desolate; as far as the eye could reach it was desolate; the bare rocks faced each other, and left a long and wide interval of thin white sand. You might wander on and look round and round, and peep into the crevices of the rocks and discover *nothing that acknowledged the influence of the seasons.* There was *no spring, no summer, no autumn;* and the winter's snow, that would have been lovely, fell *not* on these hot rocks and scorching sands. *Never* morning lark had poised himself over this desert; but the huge serpent often hissed there beneath the talons of the vulture, and the vulture screamed, his wings imprisoned within the coils of the serpent.

— From *The Wanderings of Cain*, by S. T. Coleridge.

The use of comparison is illustrated in the following paragraphs : —

She is like some tender tree, the pride and beauty of the grove; graceful in its form, bright in its foliage, but with the worm preying at its heart. We find it suddenly withering, when it should be most fresh and luxuriant. We see it drooping its branches to the earth, and shedding leaf by leaf; until, wasted and perished away, it falls, even in the stillness of the forest; and as we muse over the beautiful ruin, we strive in vain to recollect the blast or thunderbolt that could have smitten it with decay.

—From *The Broken Heart*, by Washington Irving.

A principal fruit of friendship is the ease and discharge of the fullness and swellings of the heart, which passions of all kinds do cause and induce. We know diseases of stoppings and suffocations are the most dangerous in the body, and it is not otherwise in the mind; you may take sarza to open the liver, steel to open the spleen, flower of sulphur for the lungs, castoreum for the brain; but no receipt openeth the heart but a true friend, to whom you may impart griefs, joys, fears, hopes, suspicions, counsels, and whatsoever lieth upon the heart to oppress it, in a kind of civil shrift or confession.

— Francis Bacon, Essay on Friendship.

The method of comparisons and contrasts may be used in any kind of composition. Further illustrations : —

"Take thine eyes off the bridge," said he, "and tell me if thou seest anything thou dost not comprehend." Upon looking up, — "What mean," said I, "those great flights of birds that are perpetually hovering about the bridge, and settling upon it from time to time? I see vultures, harpies, ravens, cormorants, and among many other feathered creatures, several little winged boys, that perch in great numbers upon the middle arches." — " These," said the genius, " are envy, avarice, superstition, despair, love, with the like cares and passions that infest human life."

— Joseph Addison.

Nothing strikes one more, in the race of life, than to see how many give out in the first half of the course. " Commencement day " always reminds me of the start for the " Derby," when the beautiful high-bred three-year-olds of the season are brought up for trial. That day is the start, and life is the race. . . . This is the start, and here they are, — coats bright as silk, and manes as smooth as *eau lustrale* can make them. Some of the best of the colts are pranced round, a few minutes each, to show their paces. What is that old gentleman crying about ? and the old lady by him, and the three girls, what are they all covering their eyes for ? Oh, that is *their* colt which has just been trotted upon the stage. Do they really think those little thin legs can do anything in such a slashing sweepstakes as is coming off in these next forty years ? . . .

Fifty years. Race over. All that are on the course are coming in at a walk ; no more running. Who is ahead ? Ahead ? What ! and the winning post a slab of white or gray stone standing out from that turf where there is no more jockeying or straining for victory ! Well, the world marks their places in its betting-book ; but be sure that these matter very little, if they have run as well as they know how !

— From *The Autocrat of the Breakfast Table*, by Oliver W. Holmes.
Houghton, Mifflin, and Company, by permission.

I have been up to look at the dance and supper rooms, for the inauguration ball at the Patent Office ; and I could not help thinking what a different scene they presented to my view awhile since, filled with a crowded mass of the worst wounded of the war, brought in from second Bull Run, Antietam, and Fredericksburg. To-night, beautiful women, perfumes, the violins' sweetness, the polka, and the waltz ; then the amputation, the blue face, the groan, the glassy eye of the dying, the clotted rag, the odor of wounds and blood, and many a mother's son amid strangers, passing away untended there (for the crowd of the badly hurt was great, and much for nurse to do, and much for surgeon).

— From *Specimen Days*, by Walt Whitman.
By permission.

Exercise 74. Study of paragraphs. — *Write out (a) the topic of each of the above paragraphs, (b) the kind of composition illustrated, and (c) the comparisons or contrasts made or suggested.*

Exercise 75. Making of paragraphs. — *(a) Write brief paragraphs from the following summaries, using the method of comparisons or contrasts.*

1. *The beehive.* Like a little city — the queen bee — the young — the drones — the workers — have the bees a language?

2. *Some pretend to despise what they cannot obtain.* Fable of the fox and the grapes — repeated efforts — the fox, baffled, says at last, "They are only sour grapes, anyway."

3. *Easter.* What Easter commemorates — appropriateness of the time of year — springing up of the flowers (comparison).

4. *The sunflower.* Said to turn as the sun moves (comparison) — its appearance (comparison).

5. *Troubles make men strong.* Without the need of effort we should never grow strong — comparison with an oak tree — its weak beginning — the rough winds — the hot sun — the storms — its rival trees — the strength of the great tree.

(b) When you have developed these paragraphs, give one of them orally.

IV. *Effects or results.* — We may develop a topic in a fourth way, namely, by giving the effects or results of the fact or thing used as the topic. Thus, if the topic sentence read, "The Gulf Stream is of immense importance to the civilized world," the paragraph might give many effects of the temperature and course of this ocean current. The method of effects may be used in exposition and in narration; less frequently in description and argument. (For examples of its use in description, see page 64.)

Further illustrations of this method:—

I mounted the stair. As I approached the room of which I was in search, a vapor, deadly infectious, assailed my senses. It resembled nothing of which I had ever before been sensible. Many odors had been met with, even since my arrival in the city, less supportable than this. I seemed not so much to smell, as to taste the element that now encompassed me. I felt as if I had inhaled a poisonous subtle fluid, whose power instantly bereft my stomach of all vigor. Some fatal influence seemed to seize upon my vitals, and the work of corrosion and decomposition to be busily begun.

—From *Arthur Mervyn*, by Charles Brockden Brown.

When Mr. Cooper returned in 1833, without meeting any such burst of welcome as had greeted Irving on his return the year before; and when he began shortly thereafter to scold his countrymen — in schoolmaster fashion — about their lapses from good breeding, and their lack of social independence, and their subserviency to British influences (much of which was solemnly true), the newspaper people lost their tempers and abused him loudly and continuously. This was irritating to a man who honestly believed himself better equipped to instruct and amuse his countrymen than ever before. And the irritation put him in the mood to be watchful for fresh sources of discontent. These came pretty abundantly when — after planting himself in his old remodeled home of Otsego Hall — there sprung up a fierce quarrel with his village neighbors in respect to ownership of a tongue of woodland which shot into the lake, and which had long been used as a public resort. The legal rights were with Cooper; but popular feeling all against him. What the people lacked in rights, they made up in abuse; and what the author lacked in sympathy, he made up in ill temper. The quarrel had wide echoes; slanders and libel suits ensued; Cooper winning in the courts, and losing — out of court.

> —From *American Lands and Letters*, p. 246, by Donald G. Mitchell.
> Charles Scribner's Sons, by permission.

Ambition, ruled by reason and religion, is a virtue; unchecked and maddened by vanity and covetousness, it is a vice. Without ambition, no great deed was ever accomplished. It is a guiding star to the wise and good; only a snare to the vain and foolish. Ambition is the strongest incentive to perseverance, and difficulties will sink before it, where they had appeared mountain high. It is ambition which keeps alive hope and courage. Without it, man would be content to be a poor, debased creature, allowing the powers of his brain to rest for want of energy to cultivate and apply them. He could never rise in his profession, having no ambition to reach its highest point. Like every other good gift, it is the abuse, and not the use of ambition's fire that leads to sin. Kept within the proper bounds, it is a noble quality, leading to perfection.

> — Laurence Sterne.

V. *Reasons or causes.*— A fifth way of working up a topic is to set forth reasons or causes. This method is valuable mainly in exposition and argument. It may well be used in writing on such topics as, The disappearance of the North American Indian, The benefits of giving the vote to women, The increasing frequency of strikes, Strikes do not aid the cause of labor.

Illustrations of this method:—

Let us proclaim it firmly, proclaim it even in fall and defeat, this age is the grandest of all ages; and do you know wherefore? . Because it is the most benignant. This age, the immediate issue of the French Revolution, and its first born, enfranchises the slave in America, uplifts the pariah in Asia, destroys the suttee in India, and extinguishes in Europe the last brands of the stake, civilizes Turkey, penetrates the Koran with the Gospel, dignifies woman, subordinates the right of the strongest to the right of the most just, suppresses pirates, ameliorates penal laws, purifies the galleys, throws the bloody sword into the gutter, condemns the death penalty, takes the chain and ball from the foot of the convict, abolishes torture, degrades and stigmatizes war, . . . plucks out the fangs from tyrants.

— Victor Hugo.

"Therefore," said he, "hath it with all confidence been ordered by the Commons of Great Britain, that I impeach Warren Hastings of high crimes and misdemeanors. I impeach him in the name of the Commons House of Parliament, whose trust he has betrayed. I impeach him in the name of the English nation, whose ancient honor he has sullied. I impeach him in the name of the people of India, whose rights he has trodden under foot, and whose country he has turned into a desert. Lastly, in the name of human nature itself, in the name of both sexes, in the name of every age, in the name of every rank, I impeach the common enemy and oppressor of all."

— From Macaulay's Essay on Warren Hastings.

Exercise 76. Study of paragraphs. — *After studying the paragraphs given under Methods IV and V, write out (a) the topic of each of the paragraphs, (b) the kind of composition illustrated, (c) the effects, or the causes or reasons mentioned (as the case may be).*

Exercise 77.   Writing of paragraphs. — *Write brief para-graphs on five of the following topics, developing them by giving effects, or else reasons (stating which):* —

1. Outdoor games.   2. Winter the healthfullest season.   3. The importance of forest trees.   4. The battle of Bull Run. 5. The outbreak of the Revolutionary War.   6. The drum is indispensable in battle.   7. Waves on the seashore.   8. The cold north wind.   9. A summer shower.   10. Life on a farm is pleasant.

Exercise 78.   Study of paragraphing. — *Study the follow-ing paragraphs, and determine what method of para-graph-development is used in each case. Write your answers.*

Note. — The five methods of developing paragraphs may be remembered by the aid of the keyword *picer* (particulars, in-stances, comparisons, effects, reasons).

There were, however, several persons who gave me great di-version on this occasion.   I observed one bringing in a fardel (burden) very carefully concealed under an old embroidered cloak, which, upon his throwing it into the heap, I discovered to be poverty.   Another, after a great deal of puffing, threw down his luggage, which, upon examining, I found to be his wife.

— From the Spectator Papers, by Joseph Addison.

How few men in the world are prosperous!   What an infi-nite number of slaves and beggars, of persecuted and oppressed people, fill all corners of the earth with groans, and heaven itself with weeping, prayers, and sad remembrances!   How many provinces and kingdoms are afflicted by a violent war, or made desolate by popular diseases!   Some whole countries are remarked with fatal evils or periodical sicknesses.   Grand Cairo, in Egypt, feels the plague every three years returning like a quartan ague, and destroying many thousands of per-sons.   All the inhabitants of Arabia, the desert, are in contin-ual fear of being buried in huge heaps of sand, and therefore dwell in tents and ambulatory houses, or retire to unfruitful mountains, to prolong an uneasy and wilder life.

— Jeremy Taylor.

It was a lovely drive, along winding roads rich in the picturesque scenes that delight beauty-loving eyes.   Here an ancient monastery, whence the solemn chanting of the monks came down to them.   There a bare-legged shepherd, in wooden shoes, pointed hat, and rough jacket over one shoulder, sat piping on a stone, while his goats skipped among the rocks or lay at his feet.   Meek, moss-colored donkeys, laden with panniers of freshly cut grass, passed by, with a pretty girl in a *capuline* sitting between the green piles, or an old woman spinning with a distaff as she went.   Brown, soft-eyed children ran out from the quaint stone hovels to offer nosegays, or bunches of oranges still on the bough.   Gnarled olive trees covered the hills with their dusky foliage, fruit hung golden in the orchard, and great scarlet anemones fringed the roadside; while beyond green slopes and craggy heights the maritime Alps rose sharp and white against the blue Italian sky.

Valrosa well deserved its name, for, in that climate of perpetual summer, roses blossomed everywhere.   They overhung the archway, thrust themselves between the bars of the great gate with a sweet welcome to passers-by, and lined the avenue, winding through lemon trees and feathery palms up to the villa on the hill.   Every shadowy nook, where seats invited one to stop and rest, was a mass of bloom ; every cool grotto had its marble nymph smiling from a veil of flowers, and every fountain reflected crimson, white, or pale pink roses, leaning down to smile at their own beauty.   Roses covered the walls of the house, draped the cornices, climbed the pillars, and ran riot over the balustrade of the wide terrace, whence one looked down on the sunny Mediterranean and the white-walled city on its shore.

— From *Little Women*, by Louisa M. Alcott, Ch. XXXIX.
Little, Brown, and Company, by permission.

The river (the Oise) was swollen with the long rains. From Vadencourt all the way to Origny it ran with ever-quickening speed, taking fresh heart at each mile, and racing as though it already smelt the sea. The water was yellow and turbulent, swung with an angry eddy among half-submerged willows, and made an angry clatter along stony shores. The course kept turning and turning in a narrow and well-timbered valley. Now the river would approach the side, and run gliding along the chalky base of the hill, and show us a few open colza fields among the trees. Now it would skirt the garden walls of houses, where we might catch a glimpse through a doorway, and see a priest pacing in the checkered sunlight. Again the foliage closed so thickly. in front that there seemed to be no issue; only a thicket of willows over-topped by elms and poplars, under which the river ran flush and fleet, and where a kingfisher flew past like a piece of the blue sky. . . The light sparkled golden in the dancing poplar leaves, and brought the hills into communion with our eyes. And all the while the river never stopped running or took breath, and the reeds along the whole valley stood shivering from top to toe.

*   *   *   *   *   *   *

The river was more dangerous here; it ran swifter, the eddies were more sudden and violent. All the way down we had had our fill of difficulties. Sometimes it was a weir which could be shot, sometimes one so shallow and full of stakes that we must withdraw the boats from the water and carry them round. But the chief sort of obstacle was a consequence of the late high winds. Every two or three hundred yards a tree had fallen across the river, and usually involved more than another in its fall. Often there was free water at the end, and we could steer round the leafy promontory and hear the water sucking and bubbling among the twigs. Often, again, when the tree reached from bank to bank, there was room, by lying close, to shoot through underneath, canoe and all. Sometimes it was necessary to get out upon the trunk itself and pull the boats across; and sometimes, where the stream was too impetuous for this, there was nothing for it but to land and "carry over." This made a fine series of accidents in the day's career, and kept us aware of ourselves.

— From *An Inland Voyage*, by Robert Louis Stevenson.

Nothing in the work has astonished us so much as the ignorance or the carelessness of Mr. Croker with respect to facts and dates. Many of his blunders are such as we should be surprised to hear any well-educated gentleman commit, even in conversation. . . . In one place Mr. Croker says that at the commencement of the intimacy between Dr. Johnson and Mrs. Thrale, in 1765, the lady was twenty-five years old. In other places he says that Mrs. Thrale's thirty-fifth year coincided with Dr. Johnson's seventieth. Johnson was born in 1709. If, therefore, Mrs. Thrale's thirty-fifth year coincided with Johnson's seventieth, she could have been only twenty-one years old in 1765. This is not all. Mr. Croker, in another place, assigns the year 1777 as the date of the complimentary lines which Johnson made on Mrs. Thrale's thirty-fifth birthday. If this date be correct, Mrs. Thrale must have been born in 1742, and could have been only twenty-three when her acquaintance with Johnson commenced. Mr. Croker, therefore, gives us three different statements as to her age. Two of the three must be incorrect.

— From Macaulay's Review of Croker's Boswell's Johnson.

Neither could they, with all the skill they had, get again to the stile that night. Wherefore, at last, lighting under a little shelter, they sat down there till the day brake; but, being weary, they fell asleep. Now there was, not far from the place where they lay, a castle, called Doubting Castle, the owner whereof was Giant Despair, and it was in his grounds they now were sleeping; wherefore he, getting up in the morning early, and walking up and down in his fields, caught Christian and Hopeful asleep in his grounds. Then with a grim and surly voice he bid them awake, and asked them whence they were, and what they did in his grounds. They told him they were pilgrims, and that they had lost their way. Then said the Giant, You have this night trespassed on me by trampling in and lying on my grounds, and therefore you must go along with me. So they were forced to go, because he was stronger than they.

— From *The Pilgrim's Progress*, by John Bunyan.

For do but consider what an excellent thing sleep is : it is so estimable a jewel that, if a tyrant would give his crown for an hour's slumber, it cannot be bought ; of so beautiful a shape is it, that though a man live with an empress, his heart cannot be at quiet till he leaves her embracements to be at rest with the other ; yea, so greatly are we indebted to this kinsman of death, that we owe the better tributary half of our life to him ; and there is good cause why we should do so, for sleep is that golden chain that ties health and our bodies together.

— Thomas Dekker.

Exercise 79. Topic sentences. — *Write the topic sentences of the paragraphs given in Exercise 78.*

Exercise 80. Paragraph methods. — *(a) By which methods might the following topics be developed ? (b) What kinds of compositions would be the results ? Write your answers.*

1. The game of blind man's buff.
2. How to learn to skate.
3. The robin.
4. Story of a parrot.
5. Mistakes made by poor cooks.
6. Dogs are sometimes very brave and faithful.
7. Traveling is a source of both pleasure and profit.
8. The wild flowers of spring.
9. A cat and a mouse (narrative).
10. The murder of President Garfield.

Exercise 81. Paragraph development. — *Develop into paragraphs five topics given in the last exercise, so as to have one of each type of paragraph (p. i. c. e. r.).*

Exercise 82. Writing of paragraphs. — *Develop the following summaries, according to the methods named :* —

1. *Joan of Arc.* A peasant girl in France — she sees strange visions — she goes to the king — becomes leader of the armies of France — her great victories — her capture by the English — she is burned at the stake in Rouen. (Method of particulars — narration.)

2. *The blacksmith's shop.* The blacksmith — his tools — what he is doing — the bellows, the fire, the water tub — the sparks — the finished work. (Method of particulars — description.)

3. *A friend in need is a friend indeed.* A poor Swede landed in New York, with but little money — no friends — knew not where to go — had been cheated — suddenly hears his name called — sees a friend of his boyhood in Sweden — the friend takes him to his home — the Swede gets a start — becomes prosperous. (Method of instance or example — narration.)

4. *How the world seems after a long illness.* As if one had been off on a long journey — the very sky looks strange — the people have changed — new houses have been built, etc. (Method of comparison — description.)

5. *The snow.* It falls all night — is drifted in the morning — then comes a cold snap — where the snow was blown off the plants are frozen — the thick snow covering protects the grain and the flowers (comparison) — when it melts in the spring there is a freshet. (Method of effects.)

6. *Take time by the forelock.* Miss no opportunity — we do not know what to-morrow may bring forth — a chance lost may never return — the sooner we succeed, the longer we enjoy the fruits of success. (Method of reasons.)

7. *An entertainment.* The audience — the music — the dialogues — the conjurer's tricks. (Method of particulars.)

Exercise 83. Outlining. — *Outline three of the paragraphs given in Exercise 78; or three given in the text of this chapter.*

Exercise 84. Outline for original narration. — *This exercise is in preparation for Exercise 85. Outline the narration there called for, by chief events, or places, or periods, whichever method seems best; put minor topics (subtopics) under the several head-topics. These minor topics may be descriptive, or they may be merely details of the narrative.*

Exercise 85. Narration of invented or imaginary occurrences. — *Write a ghost story, or a story of a boy's struggle for a foothold in the world, or a story of adventure or trial of some sort. Introduce some description of persons, and of places or objects. Follow your outline, developing your paragraphs with care as to their topics and their contents.*

CHAPTER X

So far, in our study of sentence making, we have had exercises on the various elements and the grammatical forms of sentences, on the securing of unity in our sentences, and on securing clearness (see Chapters IV, VI, and VIII). Now we may ask, " Very well, if we know how to make grammatical sentences that have unity and clearness, what more is necessary?" The answer is, that those things are very important, — that they are more important than anything else in making sentences, — and that it would be far better not to study anything else about sentences until we have thoroughly learned what those former chapters teach. But if we wish to become really skillful writers, there is something left to learn about sentence making, even though we write and speak correct and clear sentences. In this chapter we are to study the simplest and most useful ways of making emphatic what we wish to impress upon the minds of those who read or hear what we say.

To *emphasize* a statement, or a part of a statement, as a word or a phrase, means to call special attention to it and to impress it upon the mind. The things we say or even the words we use are not all equally im-

143

portant.   So, how shall we emphasize what we think most important ?   Sometimes writers, especially in school books, emphasize words and sentences by printing them in italics or in broad-faced type.   But in most writings (as you will see by looking at magazine articles, poems, story books, histories, and other books) the words to be made emphatic are not printed in different type from the rest.   This is because skillful writers, though they print all the words in the same type, know how to make their readers feel what is meant to be specially noticed.   There are numerous ways of doing this.   Some of them depend upon the *form* chosen for the sentence, some upon the *arrangement* of the parts of the sentence, and some upon the *wording* of the sentence.

a. *Forms of sentences, for emphasis.* — Most sentences are what are called in grammar declarative sentences, that is, they state or assert, and are closed with a period.   But many assertions may be put in the form of *a question, to which no answer is expected,* because every one knows what the answer would be ; and a question thus occurring in the midst of declarative sentences arrests our attention, and becomes more emphatic than a mere plain statement would be.   For example, —

Shall not the Judge of all the earth do right?

is much more striking than to say, —

The Judge of all the earth will do right.

So also the *exclamatory* form of sentence may be used for emphasis. It is much more striking to say, —

How dear to my heart are the scenes of my childhood!

than to say, —

The scenes of my childhood are dear to my heart.

Hence, when you are writing a series of declarative sentences and wish to call special attention to a statement, see if it would not be emphasized if put into the interrogative or the exclamatory form. These forms, however, must not be used too frequently, lest through repetition they lose their effectiveness.

Exercise 86. Transforming interrogations and exclamations. — *Change the following to declarative statements, and note how much less emphatic they become when put into the commonplace form.*

1. "How!" cried the mayor, "do you think I'll stand being treated worse than a cook?" 2. How few men in the world are prosperous! 3. When shall I find forgiveness for my sin? 4. What a fool am I, to lie thus in a dungeon when I may as well walk at liberty! 5. And as we are talking of bragging, and I am on my travels, can I forget one mighty republic, where people are always trying to pass off their claret for port? 6. Nonsense, man! Why so squeamish? Do they spare you? 7. Do these fellows never give themselves airs? 8. The sky is changed — and such a change! 9. Shall he expire, and unavenged? 10. A horse! a horse! my kingdom for a horse! 11. How they'll greet us! 12. Has the gentleman done? Has he completely done?

Exercise 87. Interrogation. — *Put the following declarations into the interrogative form. Note that in changes* *of this kind a negative question conveys the idea of an affirmative statement, and a question without a negative, the idea of a negative statement. Observe the increased emphasis given by the interrogative form.*

1. This is not your house. 2. I did not know what I was to do. 3. The happiness of peace can nowhere on earth be found. 4. Poor wretch, thy success will amount to nothing. 5. You cannot shut the windows of the sky. 6. There was never a greater surprise. 7. That is good news; you have not heard better news for this month or more. 8. Assyria, Greece, Rome, Carthage, are nothing now. 9. You would not let your little finger ache for such as these. 10. This verse shall to future ages tell thou wert my guide, philosopher, and friend. 11. The hardest thing we have to do is to learn to say, "I was mistaken, and am sorry." 12. Thy jokes, that used to set the whole table on the roar, are no more. 13. You care little for a beggar's story. It is amusing, perhaps, or you find it strange. 14. It could not be otherwise. 15. A man is not very wrong after all for being only a man.

Exercise 88. Exclamation. — *Put the following declarations into the exclamatory form. In making this change a writer may sometimes, for brevity and emphasis, omit the verb.*

1. Their melody foretells a world of merriment. 2. Ocean, I have loved thee much. 3. If this is Christian work, I should like to be a slave, along with the barbarous Turk. 4. It is sharper than a serpent's tooth to have a thankless child. 5. Sleep is an excellent thing. 6. Ah, well-a-day! I had evil looks from old and young. 7. And see those sails, they are very thin and sere. 8. I could willingly lay my head within the cold grave's silent breast. 9. Very many deeds of deathless virtue and immortal crime would ne'er have been, had the actor said, I will do this to-morrow. 10. I wish I could fitly describe that scene.

Another point worth remembering about the choice of sentence formations is that to quote directly, or use what is called *direct narration*, is more emphatic than to tell indirectly what a person said or thought. When you use direct narration you give, in quotation marks, a person's direct language. We learned, in studying clearness (page 115), that direct narration is often useful in avoiding ambiguous pronouns; it is also useful in emphasizing what some person has said.

Study the differences in the verbs and pronouns in the following examples of direct and indirect narration:

(*a*) *Direct.* — My old schoolmaster asked me: "What are you doing now, and where have you been all these years?"

Indirect. — My old schoolmaster asked me what I was doing, and where I had been all these years.

(*b*) *Direct.* — Harry's old schoolmaster asked him: "What are you doing now, and where have you been all these years?"

Indirect. — Harry's old schoolmaster asked him what he was doing now, and where he had been all these years.

(*c*) *Direct.* — Fielding says: "Without adversity a man hardly knows whether he is honest or not."

Indirect. — Fielding says that without adversity a man hardly knows whether he is honest or not.

Exercise 89. Indirect narration. — *Change the following from direct to indirect narration:* —

1. Mary said to me, at last, "Say you'll let me stay and watch you write." 2. I said to him, "You thought I was not comfortable." 3. "But I shall never try any more," said I. 4. My little boy said to me, "Papa, what do you do all day long while I am playing?" 5. You ask me, "What do you do all day?" Why, you know very well what I do. I heard your mother tell you only yesterday, "He goes down town to work, so that we may have our pleasant home." 6. Farmer Jones said to his neighbor Williams, "Your sheep are in my meadow, and I wish you would get them out."

Exercise 90. Indirect to direct narration. — *In the following sentences change the indirect report of what was said by any one, to the direct form. Be careful to use quotation marks where necessary, and to begin the quoted saying with a capital. Be sure to use pronouns and tenses of verbs precisely as you think the speaker or writer used them; give his exact language as you think it was. Note the increase in clearness and emphasis.*

1. Miss Ophelia told Tom to go for the doctor, and to lose not a moment. 2. He asked, in a low whisper, when this change had taken place. 3. Then Hopeful asked where they were now. 4. She asked him if he would call her a name she wanted him to call her. 5. One day, in much good company, I was asked whether I had seen any of their struldbrugs, or immortals. 6. He told me to look no more on the bridge, but to cast my eyes upon the thick black mist into which the tide flowed. 7. Pope said that to err is human, to forgive divine. 8. Then the other man told his brother to be of good cheer; but Christian answered that the sorrows of death had compassed him about, and he should not see the land that flows with milk and honey.

b. Order of words, for emphasis. — We have just seen that, when we are reading a series of declarative sentences, our attention is aroused if we come upon a question or an exclamation. This is because of the difference from the ordinary form of sentence. Now, for much the same reason, certain words in a sentence may be made emphatic by being placed out of their ordinary or regular position. When we say, His locks were gray, The rain came down, we use a customary arrangement, — subject, verb, complement, or modifier of the verb. Now reverse the order; say, Gray were his locks, Down came the rain, and what is the effect? In the first sentence *gray* and *locks* are both made emphatic, in the second sentence *down* and *rain* are made emphatic, all for the same reason: these words are in an *unusual* position in the sentence.

Hence, when you wish to give to a word a special emphasis, see if you cannot place it in an unusual, and yet not absurd, position. If it is the subject, put it toward or at the end of the sentence. If it is a verb, an adverb, an object element, or a predicate attribute, put it toward or at the beginning of the sentence. The two most emphatic positions in the sentence are those of the first word and the last word. Of these the more emphatic is that of the first word.

The unusual or inverted sentence arrangement must, of course, not be used too frequently. It is emphatic only when it is used occasionally.

Exercise 91.   Transposed or inverted order of words. — *In the following sentences, note what words are made emphatic by being in an unusual position, and change the sentences into the regular or natural order.*

1. Imprudent it certainly was.   2. Generously and freely did they share with you their comforts and their homes.   3. Beautiful are those lights and shadows thrown abroad among the mountains.   4. The atrocious crime of being a young man I shall not attempt to deny.   5. Much more is he to be abhorred, who has receded from virtue.   6. White as the snow were his locks, and his cheeks as brown as the oak leaves.   7. Whom, therefore, ye ignorantly worship, him declare I unto you.   8. This is the state of man: to-day he puts forth the tender leaves of hopes; to-morrow blossoms, and bears his blushing honors thick upon him; the third day comes a frost, a killing frost.   9. Across the ocean came a pilgrim bark, bearing the seeds of life and death.   10. If we do not educate, short will be our race from the cradle to the grave.

Exercise 92.   Inversion. — *Change from the usual order to the emphatic order the following sentences, by placing in emphatic positions the words which you think should be made emphatic.*

1. The church was erelong thronged with men. The women waited without in the churchyard.   2. Then their commander uprose.   3. The hope of escape was vain.   4. His tones were deep and solemn; he spake in accents measured and mournful.   5. I have labored among you forty years of my life.   6. The lamps shone bright o'er fair women and brave men.   7. I cannot do the one, and the other I will not do.   8. War had never assumed a more splendid and imposing aspect.   9. So he entered the Netherby hall boldly, among bridesmen, and kinsmen, and brothers, and all.   10. Time presses on, still on, and forever.

Another way to make words emphatic is to arrange the parts of a sentence, or of any compound element in a sentence, in pairs. This is called *balancing*, or *antithesis*. It places both the ideas in contrast, and so makes both emphatic. The two parts should be made *similar in form*.

Exercise 93. Balance and antithesis. — *What words in the following are made emphatic by contrast? In which sentences are the balanced ideas similar, and in which are they dissimilar?*

1. The mountains look on Marathon, and Marathon looks on the sea. 2. Let us be faithful to their rude virtues as men, and pay due tribute to their unhappy fate as a people. 3. The style of Dryden is capricious and varied, that of Pope cautious and uniform. 4. Dryden is read with frequent astonishment, and Pope with perpetual delight. 5. A professed Catholic, he imprisoned the Pope; a pretended patriot, he impoverished the country. 6. With one hand he smote the house of Bourbon, and wielded in the other the democracy of England. 7. Lafayette lived chiefly for his own age, and chiefly for his and our country; but Robert Raikes has lived for all ages and all countries. 8. A wise son maketh a glad father, but a foolish son is the heaviness of his mother. 9. To his equals he was condescending, to his inferiors kind. 10. If Swift's life was most wretched, I think Addison's was most enviable.

Exercise 94. Balance and antithesis. — *Make balanced sentences on the topics suggested, emphasizing either likenesses or contrasts. See that the parts are similar in form of expression.*

1. The stormy night — the calm morning.
2. To spend money — to save money.
3. Lincoln — Washington.

4. Hamilton — Benedict Arnold.
5. The violet — the peony.
6. The dog — the horse.
7. Generosity — selfishness.
8. The South during the Revolution — the North.
9. The town pump — the grog shop.
10. The poetry of Longfellow — that of Scott.

Exercise 95. Balanced construction. — *Make the corresponding parts in the following sentences similar, so as to make the balancing clear and pleasing.*

EXAMPLES: (*a*) He expected a reproof, and that his mother would punish him. (Word object balanced against clause object.)

Improved: He expected that his mother would reprove and punish him.

(*b*) He had a tall and commanding figure, and his face was strikingly handsome. (*Figure* and *face* are balanced improperly; one is an object, the other a subject.)

Improved: (make *figure* the subject in the first clause, or make *face* an object in the second clause).

1. The tears gushed from his eyes, and his face was deprived of its color. 2. He concluded that he would return home, and if his parents forgave him, he would live an honest life. 3. So faithful in love, and a dauntless warrior, there was never knight like the young Lochinvar. 4. He winds up the ascent of the stairs, and the door of the chamber is reached. 5. We delight in the bracing air of winter, and in the summer that is warm and bright. 6. To err is human, but forgiveness is divine. 7. About the river of human life there is a wintry wind, though a sunshine that is heavenly. 8. You repaid them by fraud, oppression, and conduct that was dishonorable. 9. He preferred a brisk walk across the green fields rather than to ride in the cushioned carriage. 10. He believed in one's doing

the best one knew how, and that by such a course one would become wise and happy. 11. John was told not to venture on that bridge, and, in fact, that he should not leave the yard.

When Patrick Henry said, "We have petitioned; we have remonstrated; we have prostrated ourselves at the foot of the throne," he arranged his statements in the order of their strength and proper emphasis, beginning with the weakest statement and ending with the strongest. If he had used a different order, some of the strength of his utterance would be gone. The arrangement of ideas in the order of increasing emphasis, is called *climax*.

Exercise 96. Climax. — *In the following sentences arrange the ideas in the order of climax.*

1. When shall we be stronger? Will it be when we are totally disarmed, and when a British guard shall be stationed in every house? Will it be the next week, or the next year? 2. His death-bell is tolling, black is the bier, and the war drum is muffled. 3. Must I observe you? Must I stand and crouch under your testy humor? Must I budge? 4. A tory! hustle him! a spy! away with him! a refugee! 5. If we must die, let it be under the clear sky, by the bright waters, in noble, honorable battle! If we must fight, let us fight for ourselves! If we must slaughter, let us slaughter our enemies. 6. Did I become drunk? and squabble? swear? speak parrot? swagger? 7. If you tickle us, do we not laugh? If you wrong us, shall we not revenge? If you poison us, do we not die? If you prick us, do we not bleed? 8. To be now a sensible man, presently a beast, and by and by a fool!

Somewhat similar to the principle of climax is that which tells us that the clause or statement we wish to emphasize should be placed at the end of the sentence. In the following two arrangements, see how much more emphatic the first sentence is than the second : —

O thou invisible spirit of wine, if thou hast no name to be known by, let us call thee devil ! — Shakspere.

O thou invisible spirit of wine, let us call thee devil, if thou hast no name to be known by.

So in general it is much more forcible to put the modifying phrases and clauses, as much as possible, toward the beginning, and so to put the *main statement toward or at the end.* Sentences thus formed are called *suspended or periodic.* It is not emphatic to make a statement and then add modifiers. Such a sentence is called a *loose sentence.* Loose sentences are by no means always faulty, because they avoid stiffness and the tiresomeness that would result if all the sentences were of the suspended or periodic sort. Besides, we may wish to emphasize a certain modifier ; then we should place it in an emphatic position, as at the beginning or at the end.

We should know the difference between loose and periodic sentences, and should be able easily to change one form into the other. Then we may choose, as we write, which form we need to use. In general, the periodic form, since it does not complete the main statement until at or near the end of the sentence, is the more emphatic ; while the loose form is the more familiar.

Exercise 97. Suspended structure. — *In the following sentences, rearrange the parts so as to make periodic sentences, or so as to place at the end what ought to be emphasized. Note what words are made emphatic by the rearrangement.*

1. Thou diest, and all thy goods are confiscate, if thou takest more or less than just a pound of flesh. 2. I was ill-tempered, too, when I spoke that. 3. The rank thistle nodded in the wind and the wild fox dug his hole unscared not many generations ago, where you now sit, encircled with all that exalts and embellishes civilized life. 4. The Indian hunter pursued the panting deer, beneath the same sun that rolls over your head. 5. And here curled the smoke of peace, when the tiger strife was over. 6. He still retained his good humor in this mansion of distress (a prison), though denied all amusements, and even the conveniences of life, and entirely cut off from all intercourse with his friends. 7. He called it "seeing life" whenever he fell into any misery. 8. Stand here like fat oxen waiting to be killed, if ye are beasts. Follow me if ye are men. 9. Said John, "It is my wedding day, and if I should dine at Edmonton and my wife should dine at Ware, all the world would stare." 10. Unless you are a coward, try that again. 11. And, sir, American liberty still lives, in the strength of its manhood, and full of its original spirit, where it raised its first voice, and where its youth was nurtured and sustained. 12. At the head of this vanguard rode the Bishop of Avila, upon a snow-white palfrey, followed by a long train of barefooted monks. 13. A woman sat, in unwomanly rags, plying her needle and thread, with fingers weary and worn and with eyelids heavy and red. 14. The ladies in the gallery were in a state of uncontrollable emotion, being unaccustomed to such displays of eloquence, excited by the solemnity of the occasion, and perhaps not unwilling to display their taste and sensibility. 15. At the dead hour of midnight, when all was silent in the garden, into the lock of the wicket which opened into the castle garden, the page put the key.

c. Choice of words, for emphasis. — To repeat an idea simply for the sake of filling up space, or for the reason that one has little to say, is very annoying to the reader, and very characteristic of a poor writer. To say, " The entire gallery was all lighted with brilliant lights, which were placed in every part of the room," means nothing more than that " the entire gallery was brilliantly lighted." The words " all," " with lights," " which were placed in every part of the room," are unnecessary — they really add nothing to the meaning of the sentence. Such words are said to be *redundant.*

Exercise 98. Redundancy. — *Correct the following sentences by getting rid of all unnecessary words:* —

1. He is a universal favorite among all his friends. 2. I was called upon by a poor-looking widow woman, who visited my office the other day. 3. There is an ample abundance of food here, that will serve all of us plentifully. 4. He cut the grass with a keen and sharp scythe that needed no whetting. 5. In this work we are necessarily forced to meet many difficult obstacles that will be hard for us to overcome. 6. They often benefit by it sometimes, for experience is the best teacher. 7. We must repeat the lesson over and over again.

The *repetition* of a word or of a form of expression, however, is often very emphatic. In your writing do not be afraid to repeat, therefore, provided you have the intention of making something clear and emphatic by the repetition.

Note the strong effect produced by repetition either of meaning or of language in the following passages:

1. They are meant for us; they can be meant for no other.
2. What is it that gentlemen wish?   What would they have?
3. Remember March, the ides of March remember!   4. No villain regards the Sabbath. No vicious family regards the Sabbath.   No immoral community regards the Sabbath.   5. If we wish to be free; if we mean to preserve inviolate those inestimable privileges for which we have been so long contending; if we mean not basely to abandon the noble struggle in which we have been so long engaged, we must fight! I repeat it — we must fight! An appeal to arms and the God of Hosts is all that is left us.

> 6.   Work! work! work!
>   Till the brain begins to swim;
>   Work! work! work!
>   Till the eyes are heavy and dim.
>   Seam and gusset and band,
>   Band and gusset and seam,
>   Till over the buttons I fall asleep,
>   And sew them on in a dream.

> 7. By foreign hands thy dying eyes were closed,
>   By foreign hands thy decent limbs composed,
>   By foreign hands thy humble grave adorned,
>   By strangers honored, and by strangers mourned.

We may sometimes emphasize an idea by *denying the opposite* of it. Thus, to say, " This has been no easy task," is a way of saying emphatically that the task was difficult. It has this effect because a milder statement than we expect attracts the attention and gives an impression of care and accuracy, leading us to give full weight to what *is* said. But sometimes, of course, denying the opposite makes a statement more cautious, and therefore *less* direct and emphatic.

Exercise 99. Denying the opposite. — *Change the following sentences by denying the contrary of what is said. Note whether the original or the changed sentence is the more emphatic.*

1. She is a lazy girl. 2. This was an event of great importance. 3. As I lay crouched in the hogshead, hearing the soldiers near at hand, my position was uncomfortable. 4. I am a grown man. 5. He stood still. 6. It was a very dull town (give negative particulars). 7. Just before the storm broke there was a great silence in the forest (mention sounds that were not heard). 8. It was a wretched place for a little child to be growing up (give negative particulars).

There is still another suggestion to be offered, with regard to making ideas emphatic. It is much less striking to say, —

He had but a wretched shelter all that stormy night;

than to say, —

He had but a thorn bush to huddle under all that stormy night.

The reason why the latter is more emphatic, is that the word " thorn bush " is more definite than " shelter." To illustrate again, " swallow-tail coat " is more definite than " garment," because a swallow-tail coat is one particular kind of garment. *Specific words* produce a vivid effect of reality, while general words are often vague and colorless.

Exercise 100. Specific words. — *In the following pairs of words, which are the more specific terms?*

1. Horse, animal. 2. Hopping, moving. 3. Purple, color. 4. Melancholy, state of feeling. 5. Reptile, snake. 6. Exercise, walking. 7. Food, boiled potatoes. 8. Monarch, king.

Exercise 101. Use of specific words. — *In the following sentences substitute for the italicized words others that are more specific. Note the increase in emphasis or force.*

1. As I saw a larger boy strike his playfellow, I was suddenly filled with *a strong emotion*. 2. *Burrowing animals* have holes and *creatures of the air* have nests, but the Son of Man hath not any *place to rest*. 3. Old age may sometimes be pitiful, but it cannot be so bad as *certain kinds of disease* or *some species of misfortune*. 4. His *clothes* were ragged and torn (specify the garments, with particulars). 5. He was never a studious man; what cared he for *the subjects treated of in books?* 6. I had seen many *wild animals*, but I never before was placed in a position so full of *discomfort* as this. 7. On the table were *various fruits* and two or three *dishes I was fondest of*. It was worth *being sick* three weeks to be able so to enjoy taking food again. 8. After all, *a writing instrument* is mightier than *an instrument of battle*. 9. Consider the *flowers* of the *surface of the earth*, how they grow; they toil not, neither do they *manufacture fabrics*, and yet I say unto you that no *mighty king* in all his glory was ever arrayed like one of these. 10. Men do not gather *good fruits* from *dry and unfriendly bushes*.

Exercise 102. Tabular review. — *Make in the form of a table a review of all the suggestions given in this chapter for securing emphasis.*

Exercise 103. Application of review. — *Examine one of your own compositions, and see if you can improve any sentences in any of the ways named in your review (Exercise 102). If you can add emphasis by rearrangement, by change of sentence-form, or by a better choice of words, copy out the sentences and place the improved forms beside them, thus:* —

Sentences to be improved.   Improved forms.

Exercise 104. Review of direct narration. — *Rewrite the
following passages after deciding where direct narration
might well be used. In writing direct quotations be careful as to punctuation and use of capitals.*

1. The countryman, who was of a goodly presence, then
came in, and it might be seen a thousand leagues off that he
was an honest, good soul. He asked which among them there
was the lord governor. The secretary answered that of course
it was he who was seated in the chair. The countryman said
he humbled himself in the governor's presence, and kneeling
down, he begged for his hand to kiss. Sancho refused it, and
commanded him to rise and tell his business. The countryman
did so, and said he was a husbandman, a native of Miguel
Turra.

2. I asked him if he left her the four shillings, too, which he
had said was his week's pay. He answered that he had, and
that I should hear her admit it. So he called Rachel again —
which it seems was her name — and asked her if she had
gotten the money. She said she had. He asked her how
much it was. She answered that it was four shillings and a
groat. Then praying God's blessing upon her, he turned to go
away.

3. Now, as they came to these places, behold, the gardener
stood in the way, of whom the pilgrims asked whose goodly
vineyards and gardens those were that they saw. He answered
that they were the King's, and were placed there for his
own delight, and also for the solace of pilgrims. So the
gardener led them into the vineyards and bade them refresh
themselves.

4. The merchant said he had a weakness for young men,
and though he knew the danger of disappointing his master,
the Pasha, he was unable to resist the young man's supplica-
tions. So he told him to take the necklace, but demanded
that the young man promise to give whatever he, the merchant,
might ask in exchange. The young man replied that he might
take his head itself if he wanted to, for he had saved his life.

Exercise 105. Review of interrogation and of exclamation. — *In the following passages decide which few sentences might well be made interrogatory or exclamatory, and rewrite such sentences in the desired forms :* —

1. These are the mansions of good men, he said; every island is a paradise accommodated to its inhabitants. He thought these were habitations worth contending for. Life, he said, did not appear miserable, that gave me opportunities of earning such a reward. Death was not to be feared, that would convey me to so happy an existence.

2. "Look for the knight in dark armor, fair Rebecca, and see how he bears himself ; for as the leader is, so will his followers be." "I see him not," said Rebecca. "He is a foul craven," said Ivanhoe ; "it seems he blenches from the helm when the wind blows highest." "He does not blench, he does not blench," said Rebecca ; "I see him now ; he leads a body of men close under the outer barriers."

3. The day was made for laziness, and lying on one's back in green places, and staring at the sky. This was not a time to be poring over musty books in a dark room. The idea was monstrous.

4. "I have no power to speak, sir." "I am astonished to see that you are amazed at my misfortunes. It is strange to me that you can wonder that a great man may decline."

5. Our hearts bound to the music of the solitary cries we hear in the mountains, to the tinkle of the gushing rills, to the sound of their cataracts. The odors that breathe from the upland turf, from the rock-hung flower, from the hoary and solemn pine, are very inspiriting. The transparent haze that is diffused over the valleys and the lower slopes, as over a vast picture, is very beautiful.

6. Our brethren are already in the field. There is no good reason why we should stand here idle. We cannot wish peace with dishonor. Life is not so dear, in my opinion, or peace so sweet, as to be purchased at the price of chains and slavery.

CHAPTER XI

LETTER WRITING

WHEN we consider that, for most of us, perhaps three fourths of the writing we do after leaving school is in the form of letters, we ought to take especial care to learn how to write letters in proper form and with skillful expression. Letters, of course, may contain any of the four kinds of composition, but usually they are occupied with description or narration, except in certain types of business letters. In the body of a letter dealing with several topics, we should take the same care in indention for new paragraphs as in any other form of composition.

Letters are divided into (*a*) social letters and (*b*) business letters. The first are either informal and personal, or formal. The difference here is that the informal style is more familiar and easy, employing naturally the first and second personal pronouns; while the formal style, as used often in invitations, acceptances, and regrets, is distant in manner, though of course courteous, and employs the third personal pronoun.

I. SOCIAL CORRESPONDENCE

Examples of formal notes

Mr. and Mrs. Hobart H. Vermilye request the pleasure of Mr. Davis's company at dinner, Wednesday, February sixteenth, at seven o'clock.

14 Brattle Street.

Mr. Davis regrets extremely that a previous engagement prevents his accepting Mr. and Mrs. Vermilye's kind invitation for Wednesday evening.

17 Washington Square,
February eleventh.

Will Miss Clark kindly excuse Helen's unavoidable absence yesterday from school, and oblige her mother,

KATE M. BURNETT.

124 West Fiftieth Street,
Wednesday morning.

It should be observed in reading these notes that the writer begins at once what he has to say; that the *place*, and, whenever necessary, the *date* of the writing are put after the note, at the left; that the day of the month is written out; that the year, in such notes, is usually not mentioned; and that pronouns of the first or the second person are not used. Notes meant to be formal must not contain any informal expressions. It is absurd to begin formally, in the third person, and end with "Yours very truly," or the like. Formal notes should be so arranged that no name shall be partly on one line and partly on another.

In all letters the writer should be careful to preserve a half-inch margin at the left of each page, and should not write anything within an inch or more of the top of the first page; but in formal notes much more care must be taken with regard to all margins. The spaces left blank at the top and the bottom of the page should be about equal.

In *informal* social notes or letters, the aim should be to write easily and more or less conversationally. It is sometimes difficult to make a careful description or a somewhat long narrative seem easy and unstilted. This means only that real excellence in letter writing, as in most other efforts, is none too common. The writer should at least, however, be able to choose the forms of address and of closing that are fitting. You would hardly write to a close and intimate friend with the salutation "Dear Sir" and the ending "Yours respectfully." In social letters one may choose from such *forms of salutation* as these: —

> My dear Charles:
>
> Dear Mother:
>
> Dear Uncle Henry:
>
> Dear Miss Reed:

To use "my" before "dear" in a salutation adds some formality — lessens the tone of intimacy or of cordiality.

The following are some *forms of closing* for social letters: —

Cordially yours,	Believe me, yours faith-
Yours most sincerely,	fully,
As ever, yours,	Your affectionate cousin,
Your loving son,	Your loving daughter,

Whether you should sign your full name after such forms of closing, or only your first name or a nick-name depends, of course, upon your relation to your correspondent. Do not write "Yours, etc."

In a social letter it is necessary to have the following parts : —

The heading, giving place and time of writing. This information is, except in brief informal notes (see model below), put at the top of the letter, toward the right. The place of writing must be given with sufficient detail to enable your correspondent to address his letter to you properly.

The salutation, to be placed a line below the heading, but at the left. Examples of forms of salutation have already been given.

The body of the letter.

The form of closing, toward, but not reaching to, the right-hand margin, at the end of the letter. Examples already given.

The signature.

Examples of social correspondence

1. *Informal note.*

> DEAR MRS. PATTISON:
>
> Will you have the kindness to send me, by the bearer of this note, Lanciani's "Ancient Rome"? It will be very useful to me in the preparation of my article on Roman life.
>
> Sincerely yours,
>
> 2025 Seventh Avenue,   MARION S. WRIGHT.
> Monday, Nov. 8.

2. *A letter to a friend or relative.* (Note. — As the following letter of Rossetti's does not illustrate the point, it should be noted that it is always advisable to write somewhere, even in a private letter, the full name of the person to whom the letter is written. Otherwise it may be impossible to determine afterward to whom the letter was written. The name and address may well be placed at the end, to the left.)

> 14 Chatham Place, London,
> Monday, 19 May, 1856.
>
> MY DEAR AUNT CHARLOTTE:
>
> I will certainly paint Aunt Eliza for you as soon as she comes to town. It will not be any great tax on my time, as a portrait is a thing needing no forethought, and to be taken up at any moment.
>
> If Lady Bath wishes to favor me with a visit, the best time would be now, as I happen to have two or

three things just finished, still by me — especially a drawing from Dante's "Vita Nuova," which I should have much pleasure in showing her. It is better worth seeing than "The Monk," which is not yet finished, but which I could show her also. I should also very much like to show *you* the things, if you come with Lady Bath, supposing she is able to give me that pleasure.

Your affectionate nephew,

D. G. ROSSETTI.

Exercise 106. Formal notes. — (*a*) *Write a formal note, inviting a friend to a luncheon.* (*b*) *Write an acceptance of the invitation.* (*c*) *Write a note of regret in response to an invitation to a wedding.*

Exercise 107. Informal notes. — (*a*) *Write a note, acknowledging the receipt of a Christmas present.* (*b*) *Write a note to a friend, to thank him for the use of a book which you are returning. Mention the book by name, and give your opinion of it.* (*c*) *Write a note to a friend, asking him to meet you at a certain time and place, and stating the purpose of the meeting.* (*d*) *Write a note introducing one of your friends to a person residing in a city which your friend is about to visit.*

In *addressing the envelope* of a letter, observe the following suggestions : —

I. The *name* of the person addressed should usually be preceded by *Miss, Mrs.,* or *Mr.,* as the case may be. In addressing a minister or a doctor, use such a form as *Rev.* S. C. Burgess or *Dr.* Charles Probasco. Do not give, in such cases, the last name only. In addressing lawyers and perhaps some other classes of men, instead of *Mr.* before the name, *Esq.* may be written after it. The title *Hon.* is appropriate only to a Congressman, a Judge, or other public official. In addressing a business firm, the title *Messrs.* is frequently used when the firm name includes the names of persons, as Messrs. Brown, Johnston, and Company. Of course one would not write " Messrs. American Book Company."

2. The *direction* of the letter to street and number (when necessary), city or town, and State, should follow below the name of the person or firm addressed, and should be placed as in the models given on the next page. The name of the city or town and that of the State may be written on the same line. As a rule, the names of States should not be abbreviated. The post office box number, if it is necessary to use it in the address, may be placed toward the lower left-hand corner of the envelope. If the letter is important, the name and address of the sender should be given on the upper left-hand corner. In addressing a letter of introduction (see Exercise 107, *d*), it is customary to write in the lower left-hand part of the envelope the form of words, " *Introducing Mr. Charles E. Smalley.*"

What is written on the envelope is called the *superscription. No punctuation marks* need be used at the ends of the lines in the superscription, except to mark abbreviations. The *stamp* should always be placed in the upper right-hand corner.

Examples of superscriptions

Miss Clara Middleton
56 Pike's Peak Avenue
Denver, Colorado

2 cent
stamp

From A. B. See,
Oberlin, Ohio, U.S.A.

5 cent
stamp

Messrs. David Copperfield & Co.
152-154 Strand
London
England

II. BUSINESS LETTERS are arranged according to the following example: —

312 Ohio Avenue,

CINCINNATI, OHIO, July 3, 1896.

MR. EVAN HARRINGTON,
12 West 2d Street, New York.

DEAR SIR; — The clothing recently sent me by you (shipped June 21) is of such inferior quality that I am unwilling to offer it to my customers. Your house has always dealt fairly with me heretofore, but I am obliged to advise you that the recent shipment is wholly unsatisfactory, and will be laid aside until your directions regarding it are received. An immediate reply will be a favor to

Yours respectfully,

NICHOLAS NICKLEBY.

It will be noted that in this form of letter not only are the parts used in the social letter given, — the heading, the salutation, the body of the letter, the form of closing, and the signature, — but the *name and address* of the firm or person to whom the letter is written, are placed above the salutation. Sometimes, perhaps less formally, these are placed after the letter, toward the left, on the lines below the signature, as in the next following letter.

In business letters to women, whether married or unmarried, the form of salutation is " Dear Madam." To men the usual form is " Dear Sir " or " Dear

Sirs." For the latter, "Gentlemen" is sometimes used. "Madam," "Sir" or "Sirs" is purely formal.

Women, in signing a letter, should write in parentheses Mrs. or Miss, as the case may be. A married woman, after signing her own name in full, should add, in parentheses, Mrs., followed by her husband's name; thus,

Very truly yours,

Amelia J. Clark

(Mrs. John *K*. Clark).

Business letters should be as brief as possible, consistently with clearness. A fault in the letter of Mr. Nickleby, given above, is that he does not state what was the matter with the clothing of which he complains. Mr. Harrington would naturally have to write a letter to inquire about this, and so time would be lost because of the faulty brevity in the first letter.

Another important suggestion to the writer of business letters is, that *in replying* to a letter one should in every case state briefly the contents of that letter. By doing this, one not only saves the time of one's correspondent, but prevents misunderstanding. It may be unnecessary to summarize the entire letter before beginning the reply itself, but at least the important points, or those to which the reply is directed, should be stated. This is illustrated in the following letter : —

1879 West 206th Street,

CHICAGO, ILLINOIS, May 2, 1900.

DEAR MADAM :

In reply to your letter of April 29th, in which you complain that the articles recently purchased by you had not been delivered by us, and that your letter was the second you had written to us on the subject, we beg to assure you that no letter from you of earlier date than April 29th has been received by us. We have lost no time in seeking to discover the error of which you apprise us, and now have pleasure in informing you that we have succeeded in tracing and recovering the missing articles, which had been sent to a wrong address. They will, we trust, reach you to-morrow. With apologies for the much regretted delay,

We remain truly yours,

TARQUE AND PILFORD,

MISS ISABEL C. HENRY,   per J. McK.

25 Irving Place, Indianapolis.

One or two other suggestions regarding business correspondence : —

While a business letter should be brief and to the point, it is a matter both of courtesy and of good practice *not to use clipped forms* of words or sentences. Avoid, therefore, abbreviations such as " rec'd," " y'rs "; and do not omit the subjects of your sentences, as, " Have written to Chicago headquarters."

When you reply to a letter, state the date of that letter. Some business firms request correspondents in replying to " refer to this letter as B 210," or the like. The point is to make it perfectly plain to what letter you are replying, so that your correspondent may easily find it in his files.

It is advisable in addressing a large office or establishment with several departments, to write a distinct letter concerning each of the unrelated matters of your correspondence, so that each letter may be received and filed by the proper department.

Exercise 108. Business letters.

Note. — It is of the utmost importance in business letters that they be properly divided into paragraphs. If several topics are to be spoken of, they should be kept perfectly distinct. The best plan is to note down the topics before writing the letter. In replying to a letter covering two or more points, the distinctness of these points should be recognized by the paragraphing.

1. Write a letter from Oliver Twist, Pawtucket, Rhode Island, inclosing $4 to Harper and Brothers, Franklin Square, New York, for his subscription for one year to *Harper's Weekly.*

2. Write a letter from Henry Esmond, applying for a position as clerk in a bank. Age, experience, and references should be given.

3. Write a letter to Edward March, publisher of the *Weekly Mirror*, 17 West 31st Street, Brooklyn, New York, asking to have the address of your paper changed. In such a letter you must give both the old and the new address.

4. Write to the American Book Company, ordering fifty copies of this book, inclosing a money order, and directing how the books are to be sent, and where.

5. Write an answer for the American Book Company to the last letter.

6. Write to a gas company, inclosing their bill, with your check for the amount, and complaining that the gas is of poor quality.

7. Mrs. Rebecca S. Crawley, wife of Rawdon Crawley, of 10 Poppenham Terrace, is asked by a former servant to write a letter of recommendation. Write the letter.

8. Write a letter to your teacher, asking for a letter of recommendation, as you are obliged to leave school, and have a chance of employment in a situation for which you believe you are fitted.

9. Write a letter to John Havemeyer and Co., calling their attention to three errors in a bill recently sent you for various purchases, and asking them to correct these errors on the bill.

10. Write a letter to the school committee, or board of education, asking that no school be held on the Friday after Thanksgiving, and stating three reasons why the petition should be granted. This letter should be signed by several persons.

Exercise 109. Letters from outlines. — *Where, in the following letters, the matter is descriptive, take care to introduce your own feelings and sense-impressions; where the matter is narrative, endeavor to make it interesting by reason of the characters or situations of the persons, and the nature of the places and incidents. Attend carefully to the paragraphing.*

1. (From a boy on a visit in a strange city. To his parents.)
Arrived two days ago — the trip — arrival — meeting at the station — the host's home — went to theater the first evening — opinion of the play — the doings of the next day — places visited — plans — impressions of the city.

2. (From a girl to her school friend. During summer vacation.)
Time of leaving home — the journey — description of summering place — occupations — places of interest — persons met — plan for the remainder of summer.

3. (From a boy who has just entered into business life. To his uncle.)

How he got his position — nature of his duties — difficulties — how he is treated — life outside of working hours — remembrances to uncle and family.

4. (A letter to a friend who is absent for a year in Europe.)

Kind of time you suppose your friend is having — how things are going on at home — school — incidents — news about friends — questions concerning Europe — hope for a prompt and a long reply.

5. (A letter describing a visit to Concord, Mass.)

By train from Boston — memories of the march of the British in 1775 — the quietness of Concord — its frame houses and big elm trees — Emerson's home, outside and inside — The Wayside, once dwelt in by Hawthorne — his tower — his walk on the piny hillside — the little schoolhouse of Bronson Alcott — the home of Thoreau — The Old Manse — the Concord River, the bridge, the statue commemorating the battle — the cemetery where the famous men lie buried — reflections about the history of this little village.

6. (From a boy, describing to a friend a recent game of baseball.)

The weather — the two teams — prominent members — the beginning — description of two or three exciting times in the game — the result.

7. (Letter describing your seeing and hearing some famous man.)

How it came about — the crowd present — your first impression — what he said — his manner — why he became famous, as you suppose.

8. (Letter in reply to a friend who prefers living in the country.)

Admit the advantages of the country, especially in summer — name them — point out the advantages of the city over the country.

9. (Letter from a man of thirty to a man he has not heard from for fifteen years.)

At school together — those old days — leaving that school — further education — family events — first position — subsequent positions — travels — married? — prospects — inquiries about his friend.

10. (Letter describing winter, to a child who lives in southern California.)

The winds — the temperature — the frozen ground — the ice — skating — snow — sledding — other sports — effect of winter upon health and strength — what you suppose life is like in a climate where there is no winter.

Exercise 110. Kinds of composition. — *What kinds of composition are called for in the letters of the last exercise?*

Exercise 111. Outlining. — *Outline in full one of the letters in Exercise 109, with topics and subtopics properly arranged. If necessary, correct the paragraphing in your letter by the aid of the outline. Note whether your own letters and those of your classmates possess completeness, unity, and plan.*

Exercise 112. Sentence-criticism. — *Read over carefully one or more (as the teacher may direct) of the letters written by your classmates. Suggest in the margin corrections in spelling, punctuation, and paragraphing; mark with " U " sentences which you think lack unity or contain misuse of "and"; with " Cl " sentences lacking clearness, by reason of faulty use of pronouns or misplacing of modifiers; and with " F " sentences which you think might be made more emphatic by a rearrangement or by other change in expression.*

CHAPTER XII

ALONG with the means of emphasis already treated of in Chapter X, we should consider one more, which is very important, the use of what are called figures of speech. There are certain forms of expression which may give not only emphasis, but also clearness and beauty to what we say. Some figures, in fact, are used merely for the sake of their beauty; but usually they also add force to the expression of the idea. We shall consider only a few of the commoner and more useful figures here. A full treatment of the subject belongs only to an advanced work on rhetoric.

I. *Simile.* — If we wish to say that the Assyrian enemy came down upon the city *secretly* and *fiercely*, we may express both these ideas with vividness and therefore with emphasis by using such a comparison as this : —

The Assyrian came down like a wolf on the fold.— Byron

In this too the swiftness, devouringness of the wolflike Assyrians, give you, on the other hand, the panic, rout, unresistingness of the sheep.

A comparison of this sort is called a *simile.* It is always plainly marked as a comparison by the use of

such words as *like, as, than, resembles,* etc.   A simile
is not a comparison of things of the same sort, as one
man with another.   Thus, the sentence, " Napoleon
was a greater general than Cæsar," is a mere comparison, not a simile ; or to say, " This flower looks
like a rose," is not to use a simile.   A simile, then,
is an *expressed comparison between objects of different*
kinds.   The reason why a simile adds clearness and
vividness to our writing is that it brings up something common, familiar, or concrete to explain that
which we wish our readers to see or feel.   By the
use of a simile we thus tell or hint to our readers
that what we are writing about, which perhaps they
have not seen or may not imagine vividly, is like
something they *have* seen, or know about, or can
picture.

A simile fully stated forms what is called a proportion — A : B : : C : D.   Thus, —

Their ranks were breaking like thin clouds before a Biscay
gale,

could be stated more fully, —

As thin *clouds* break before a *gale,* so their *ranks* broke before
the onset of the *enemy.*

Note that, while a simile is a comparison between
unlike objects, yet there must of course be one or
more points of *likeness,* and these are precisely what
the simile brings out and emphasizes.   Thus, in the
last simile quoted, in what respect were the ranks of
the defeated army like clouds ?   Of course not in color

or texture or weight, or, in fact, in any respect except that of helplessly breaking and yielding to a force. A simile such as this adds not only emphasis but clearness and beauty to the statement.

Exercise 113. Simile. — *Examine the following similes, then (a) tell wherein the resemblance lies; (b) state the simile in full, as a proportion.*

1. Fret not thyself because of evil doers, for they shall be cut down like the grass, and wither as the green herb. — Bible. 2. It seems to me those verses shine like the stars. — Thackeray. 3. Troubled thoughts filled his mind as if with a fog. — Balzac. 4. He was carried about from place to place like a bale of goods; he never moved, and he said nothing. 5. Meanwhile in the old State House, dim as ghosts, sat the lawgivers of Connecticut. — Whittier. 6· If reasons were as plentiful as blackberries, I would give no man a reason on compulsion. — Shakspere's *Henry IV.* 7. Stones and beams are hailed down on the brave champion; he regards them no more than if they were thistle down and feathers. — Scott. 8. Every phrase was a calamity like the blows of a bludgeon. — Balzac. 9. The first time I read an excellent book, it is to me just as if I had gained a new friend. — Goldsmith. 10. He received my arguments with his mouth open, like a poorbox gaping for half-pence, and, good or bad, he swallowed them all without any resistance. — Colman. 11. High o'er the heads of the others rose, with his arms uplifted, the figure of Basil the blacksmith, as, on a stormy sea, a spar is tossed by the billows. — Longfellow. 12. O Cassius, thou art yokèd with a lamb, that carries anger as the flint bears fire, who, much enforcèd, shows a hasty spark, and straight is cold again. — Shakspere's *Julius Cæsar.* 13. This juggler would catch four balls in succession, in less than a second of time, and make them revolve around him at certain intervals, like the planets in their spheres; would make them chase one another like sparkles of fire, or

shoot up like flowers or meteors ; would throw them behind his back, and twine them round his neck like ribbons, or like serpents. — Hazlitt.

A simile should always be chosen and expressed with good judgment. An inappropriate simile is worse than none. If you are describing a person whom you do not wish to make ridiculous, it would not be well to say that in dodging the attacks of enemies he jumped about like a monkey. This might be perfectly true, but the comparison would be ill chosen. You should also have some regard to size and form, as well as to fittingness of suggestion. You might well enough say, " The farmer's cheeks were as ruddy as rosy-cheeked apples," but hardly would it do to say, " His cheeks were as ruddy as his barn, newly painted red."

If you wish to make your similes pleasing, do not make them too short and simple, or too commonplace. Such expressions as " black as coal," " red as fire," are worn out. Longfellow does not say merely, " Her eyes were black as berries," but he makes the comparison particular and beautiful, " Black were her eyes as the berry that grows on the thorn by the wayside." The more fullness and definiteness the better. To say " He fled before his enemies as a leaf before the wind," is not so good as to say " He fled swiftly, blown by the blast of fate, like a dead leaf over a frozen meadow."

The way to make a fine simile is not by thinking of words, but by fixing your mind upon the object, event, or person to be described, or the characteristic to be illustrated. Ask yourself, What is this like? and let the images come.

Exercise 114. Simile. — *Work out appropriate similes as suggested.*

1. The gates once being open, our men poured into the town like . . .

2. Life bears us on like . . .

3. Books are to the mind what . . .

4. At this period of his life he enjoyed a prosperity that was as . . .

5. Smoothly out of the harbor, with all sails set, the ship came . . .

6. War passed over the land like . . . leaving devastation behind it.

7. As he said this, the man's eyes . . .

8. Wit, sudden gleams; kindly humor, steady glow of light.

9. I saw the moon's bright reflection in the waters under me, like . . .

10. Eloquence comes, if it comes at all, like the . . .

II. *Metaphor.* — If, instead of saying, "She waited, like an ill-tempered cat, to give him with her sharp words a parting scratch as he went out," we leave out the words that express the comparison of the person to a cat, and say, "She waited to give him with her sharp words a parting scratch as he went out," we save time and gain emphasis by merely *suggesting* the person's likeness to a cat. In like manner, the simile, " Thy words are as a lamp to my feet," may be shortened and at the same time strengthened by omitting " as." Of course it is

absurd to speak of words as actually scratching a
person, or of words as actually being a lamp. When
we read such an expression we understand that the
writer means to suggest a comparison. The difference between a simile and this second kind of figure,
called *metaphor*, is that the latter is an *implied or
suggested comparison.*

Exercise 115. Metaphor. — *Examine each of the following metaphors, then (a) tell wherein the resemblance
lies; (b) state the comparison in full, as a proportion.*

1. "Twenty-five thousand francs!" cried César, feeling ice
in his veins instead of blood. — Balzac. 2. He was now in the
turbulent and seething city, which a modern poet has called a
vat. 3. Open that rusty door of your mouth, and make your
ugly voice walk out of it. — Colman. 4. The earth is the cup,
the sky is the cover, of the immense bounty of nature. —
Emerson. 5. Misfortune is a stepping-stone for genius, a
treasure for the skillful man, an abyss for the feeble. — Balzac.
6. Dryden's page is a natural field, rising into inequalities
and diversified by varied vegetation; Pope's is the velvet
lawn, shaven by the scythe, and leveled by the roller. —
Johnson. 7. I have but one lamp by which my feet are
guided, and that is the lamp of experience. — P. Henry.
8. Poverty froze the genial current of his soul. 9. Say that
Wolsey, who sounded all the depths and shoals of honor,
found thee a way, out of his wreck, to rise in. 10. His
conversation was uninteresting; it was weak water gruel
—a tame rabbit, boiled to rags, without sauce or salt. —
Colman.

Exercise 116. Metaphors to similes. — *By introducing
"like," "as," or other words expressing comparison,
change the metaphors quoted in Exercise 115 into
similes. Note the loss in brevity and force.*

Exercise 117. Similes to metaphors. — *By omitting all expression of the comparisons, change the similes in Exercise 113 to metaphors. Note the greater condensation, but also, in some cases, a loss in clearness.*

Simile and metaphor are the two chief figures that one should try to learn to use. It is not well to employ many figures in one's writing, at least not until one is wise enough to exercise good judgment as to the number and character of them; though of course it is good that a writer use any kind of figure that comes naturally to him and helps him to express his idea or his feeling. It is, moreover, important to be able to recognize several other figures of speech besides simile and metaphor, so that we may enjoy them when we meet them in reading. Some of the additional figures which it is well to understand are now to be briefly explained and illustrated.

III. *Personification.* — Sometimes we speak of things not living as though they were alive. This may be either because they at the time seem alive, or because we can make the idea of them emphatic by ascribing life to them. Thus, the idea of Rome is made more stately and beautiful by using this figure of *personification :* —

" This is Rome, that sat on her seven hills, and from her throne of beauty ruled the world." — Mitford.

Personification may merely give feeling to inanimate things or vegetable life, as, " The mountain shuddered," " The branches moaned in the wind "; or it may give to inanimate things or to plants or to lower animals human qualities, as, "Then would the very stones of the street rise and mutiny." Animals may shudder or moan, but only men can mutiny. Personification, then, ascribes to its object qualities of something *higher than itself* in the scale of being.

Exercise 118. Personification. — *Examine the following sentences for examples of personification, state why the figure is personification, and give a reason for the writer's having used this figure.*

1. Then, too, the old year dieth, and the forests utter a moan. — Longfellow. 2. Hope for a season bade the earth farewell, and Freedom shrieked when Kosciusko fell. 3. Let the dead past bury its dead. 4. Soon as the evening shades prevail, the moon takes up the wondrous tale, and nightly to the listening earth repeats the story of her birth. — Addison. 5. Hear me, ye walls, that echoed to the tread of either Brutus, once again I swear the eternal city shall be free. — Mitford.

IV. *Metonymy and synecdoche.* — Personification, like metaphor and simile, may be said to depend on a resemblance, real or imaginary. In fact, all personifications are really metaphors. But if we say, "This dish is well cooked," we mean, the *food* in the dish is well cooked. There is *no resemblance* between the dish and the food, but there is so usual a *connection* between them that we may speak of the dish when we really mean what is in the dish. A *metonymy* is the using of one word in place of another, when the two ideas are closely and commonly con-

nected.   When the connection between the two ideas
is that of *part* and *whole,* the figure is called *synecdoche;* for example, " He employs twelve *hands* in
his factory."

Exercise 119.   Metonymy and synecdoche. — *Point out
the instances of metonymy and of synecdoche in the following sentences, and tell what the words used in the
figures are really substituted for, and what the connections are between the ideas.*

1. No sheltering roof was nigh.   2. He wielded the scepter
for fully twenty years.   3. Do you read Shakspere?   4. He
is the worst oar in the crew.   5. She was by now a maiden of
sixteen summers.   6. The hedges are white with May.   7. All
the world looked on indifferently.   8. A fleet of twenty sail
came out of the west.   9. He is a slave to his pipe.   10. I
have always voted for the administration.

V.   *Allegory.* — An allegory is a series of metaphors,
or an extended comparison, forming a narrative.   Examples of allegory, parable, and fable, are the following : " I am the vine and ye are the branches," etc.
(St. John, Chapter xv), The parable of the prodigal
son (St. Luke xv. 11–32), Bunyan's *The Pilgrim's
Progress,* Æsop's Fables.

VI.   *Alliteration* is the use of two or more prominent words near together, beginning with the same
sound.   This is frequent in poetry, but should be
used very sparingly in prose.   Examples : " And the
sails did sigh like sedge," " Some days must be dark
and dreary," " Up the high hill he heaves a huge
round stone."

VII. *Onomatopoeia* is the use of words whose sound suggests or imitates the meaning. Words like buzz, hum, rustle, splash, flop, dinging, twang, clatter, and the like, are onomatopoetic. Onomatopoeia is frequently found in connection with alliteration.

Exercise 120. Criticism. — *Examine carefully such of your own or of your classmates' written paragraphs or longer compositions as the teacher may direct; mark in the margin with " F " sentences which you believe could be made more emphatic by rearrangement or by change of wording; and write out on a slip of paper the improved forms which you think these sentences ought to have.*

Exercise 121. Figures of speech. — *Look over two of your own exercises in paragraph-writing or in longer composition, and insert in each, in red ink, between the lines, one or two appropriate and helpful similes or metaphors.*

CHAPTER XIII

CHOICE OF WORDS

MOST of our sentence work up to this point has had to do with the form of the sentence as a whole, or with the form or arrangement of the elements of the sentence. (See the Table of Contents.) It is true that in some cases we have considered the use of certain words, namely, conjunctives, especially *and*, and the relative pronoun *which*. But in English the choice of what words we shall use is a large subject, to which whole books have been given. For the sake of learning to write more effectively, we must now study the subject a little further.

Some words and constructions ought never to be used. It may be that the words themselves are not good English, or that they are used in a wrong sense, or that they are put together ungrammatically.

I. *Correctness in diction and syntax.*

(*a.*) The words we speak or write should be in good use. This means that we must avoid : —

(1) All *slang* and vulgar expressions, such as ain't, gent, pants, photo, party (for person), well posted (for "well informed"), put it through, gave himself away, got left.

187

(2) All *local or provincial* uses of words, such as tote, onto, reckon (for " think "), be you (for "are you"), complected, like (for "as," as in the sentences, " Do like I do," " She spoke just like my mother used to speak " ; remember that when the noun or pronoun following *like* is the subject of a verb, you should use *as* instead of *like*).

(3) All *obsolete* or disused words, such as, verily, methinks.

(4) All *too recent* or as yet unaccepted words, as burglarize, motorneer, electrocute, suicided (verb).

(5) All words belonging only to *poetry*, as ere, e'er, o'er, ne'er.

(b.) We must not give to words distinctly *wrong meanings*. To illustrate : a place may be *healthful*, a certain food may be *wholesome*, but neither a place nor a food can be *healthy*, because it is not alive.

Exercise 122. Precision in use of words. — *If you are in any doubt as to the precise meaning of any of the following words, look them up in a good dictionary. The words in these groups are often used incorrectly one for another. Whether you need to look them up or not, write sentences containing these words used correctly.*

1. Accept, except (verb). 2. Balance, remainder. 3. Respectively, respectfully. 4. Invention, discovery. 5. Observation, observance. 6. Affect, effect. 7. Aggravate, irritate. 8. Demean, degrade. 9. Guess, think. 10. Lie, lay. 11. Sit, set. 12. May, can. 13. Liable, likely. 14. In, into. 15. Most, mostly, almost. 16. Like, as. 17. Quantity, number, amount. 18. Expect, suspect, suppose. 19. Quite, rather, somewhat. 20. Propose, purpose (verb). 21. Are finished, have finished.

22. To find, to found. 23. I shall, I will, he shall, he will, shall you? will you? will he? shall he? shall I? will I? (see the following note). 24. Which, that, who, whom (see the note below, on relative pronouns).

Note on "shall" and "will." — In declarative sentences, with the first person *will* expresses intention or determination; *shall* expresses merely the future tense.· With the second and third persons *will* expresses merely the future tense, while *shall* expresses intention or determination *on the part of* the speaker.

In questions, the above uses are changed, because of the answers expected. The word of the question is the word of the expected answer. Thus, *shall you?* (answer expected, I shall, or I shall not) has merely the future idea ; *will you?* asks for determined assent, the desired answer being, I will. *Will he?* is merely future, asks for information. *Shall he?* means "Do you insist or intend that he shall?" *Will I?* is usually ironical. Asked seriously, it is absurd. *Shall I?* expresses an offer, or else a mere question in the future tense.

The use of *should* and *would* is generally governed by the same rules as those for *shall* and *will*.

Note on relative pronouns. — Compare " Young birds that cannot fly are frequently starved to death " and " Young birds, which cannot fly, are frequently starved to death." In the former sentence the relative clause " that cannot fly " *limits* the antecedent " young birds." That sentence does not say that all

young birds are frequently starved to death, but
speaks only of those young birds that cannot fly.
But the second sentence says that young birds are
frequently starved to death, and adds the information
that young birds cannot fly. Here the relative
clause, since it introduces a new fact about the antecedent, is said to be *coördinative*, and may be regarded as parenthetical. The correct punctuation
also indicates this.

As a rule the pronoun *that* is used to limit or *restrict*
the antecedent; for example, in the case given, we are
not speaking of the antecedent in general (young
birds), but of a particular class of the antecedent.
To test whether a relative is used restrictively or
coördinatively in a sentence, see whether such words
as *the, that, those, that class of, those particular*, can
be or are used before the antecedent; if so, the relative is restrictive. Another test is to see whether
the relative clause is equivalent to *and he, and it, and
they*, etc., or *for he, for it*, etc., or to some other clause
which adds a new statement about the antecedent.
In such cases the clause is coördinative. To express
restriction *who, whom* and *which* are sometimes used
instead of *that* when it sounds better; as when *that* has
already been used as an adjective or a conjunction,
or when the use of *that* would throw a preposition to
the end of the sentence with an unpleasing effect.

Exercise 123. Use of relatives *who, whom, which, that*. —
*In the following sentences select the proper relative to
insert in each space. State whether the relative clause*

restricts the antecedent or merely adds information about it. Punctuate the sentences properly.

1. He is the very man . . . threw the stone. 2. We should take good care of books . . . are among our best friends. 3. Grass . . . stays green later in the year than most vegetation is a hardy plant. 4. Coal-oil lamps . . . are very cheap are now found in many houses. 5. Good shoes . . . are made of calfskin are commoner now than ever before. 6. Squirrels . . . build nests of dry leaves and twigs store up nuts for winter food. 7. He says that that is a statement . . . you may believe or not as you think best. 8. Alice in Wonderland . . . is called a children's book is much read by grown people too. 9. He believed that the stories . . . children read are often the cause of a loss of time . . . is much to be regretted. 10. That is the Mr. Phelps . . . you wanted to be introduced to. He is a man . . . I have the highest regard and admiration for.

Exercise 124. Use of *shall* and *will*. — *In the following sentences, choose from the words given in parentheses, and state the reason for your choice. If either might be used, state the difference in the meanings.*

1. I (shall, will) see him at once, or know the reason why. 2. (Should, would) you think of going to that lecture to-day? 3. I (will, shall) go up to the house at once and see what is the matter. 4. He (will, shall) do as I say, never fear. 5. (Shall, will) you not remain here till I return? 6. I am determined that this game (will, shall) be the last one I play to-day. 7. I am now at Brampton, where I (shall, will) remain all summer. 8. The count came riding up, crying, "I (will, shall) not surrender, except to death." 9. You (will, shall) not find it easy to hoodwink that lonely old man. 10. He replied scornfully, "(Shall, will) I consent to such a proposition? Never while life (will, shall) last!" 11. You (shall, will) not have the chance to do that again, so long as I

(shall, will) be here to prevent you. 12. He asked me if I (would, should) have a rehearsal that day or the next. 13. Yes, we (would, should) linger that one night till the sunrise itself (should, would) come to bid us seek our rest. 14. We (would, should) often remain till the stars came out. 15. You (should, would) not say so, if you knew him better.

(*c.*) *Correctness in syntax*, or grammatical construction of sentences, includes so much that only a few important points will be considered here, and those must be points that belong especially to the study of composition.

1. *Incorrect use of "and which."* —Since *which* is a relative pronoun, it does not require a conjunction before it, as relatives are also connectives (see page 86). It is therefore bad grammar to use *and*, *but*, *or*, or other conjunctions before *which*, *who*, or *that*, except to connect two relative clauses *having the same antecedent.* Coördinating conjunctions should always connect like elements.

EXAMPLES:

Incorrect	*Corrected*
1. He was a man of great firmness and who never could endure opposition.	1. Omit the *and* (comma after " firmness "), or recast: He was a man that was as firm as he was intolerant of opposition.
2. This is a time not meant for angry disputes, but for the right use of which we shall be held accountable.	2. This is a time which we must not spend in angry disputes, but which we must use rightly and wisely. ˙

3. This time the gateman was a man named Watty, or who was called that by his companions.

3. This time the gateman was a man whose name was Watty, or who was at any rate called that by his companions; or, This time the gateman was a man named Watty, or known by that nickname among his companions.

4. Going down the steps I met Robert Longacre, the son of a well-known writer, and whom I had never been introduced to.

4. Going down the steps I met the son of a well-known writer. It was Robert Longacre, a young man to whom I had never been introduced.

5. I believed he had the strength of a horse or an ox, but which he carefully concealed from me.

5. Though he carefully concealed the fact from me, I believed he had the strength of a horse or an ox.

6. No person unable to read, or who does not understand the Constitution, may vote in this State.

6. No person who is unable to read, or who does not understand the Constitution may vote in this State.

2. *Faults relating to possessives.* — The possessive case should be used before a gerund (verbal noun) in cases like these: "I was glad of *your* being able to make the journey, but disappointed at your *sister's* having been too ill." The use of the objective case instead of the possessive in such sentences is incorrect. For instance, to use *sister* in the sentence given would make it object of *at*, which would be absurd. Care must be taken also to write the possessive case correctly, particularly in case of compound expressions. (See Appendix III, page 239; and Maxwell's *Advanced Lessons in English Grammar*, §§ 201–208.)

Exercise 125. Use of possessive case. — *Correct the errors in the following sentences, with regard to the use, and the proper writing, of possessives.*

1. I did not like him saying that before all the others. 2. My father thinks that Lyon's and Fourpaw's circus is better than this coming one. 3. Is that Worcester or Webster's dictionary? 4. We are much obliged for Mr. Beeman having acted so promptly. 5. I have read several of Tennyson and Longfellow's poems to-day. 6. You arriving on time was what saved the day. 7. I found him at Howe's and Hubbard's law office. 8. As for your mother giving her consent, that is unlikely.

3. *Pronoun not agreeing with antecedent.* — The pronoun *they* (their, them) should generally not be used except with a plural antecedent. If the antecedent is singular and the gender unknown, better use requires that the pronoun *he*, not *they*, should be used. Thus, instead of saying, "If any one in the room has lost a handkerchief, they may obtain it after the meeting," we should say, "*he* may obtain it." We must also observe that *one, each, either*, etc., are singular, not plural, and should be referred to by *he*, not *they*. (See examples in the following exercise.)

4. *Pronouns in the wrong case-form.* — The following are common errors in the forms of pronouns: —

(*a*) Wrong case-form in questions, as, Who did you take me to be? Who are you making that for?

(*b*) Wrong case-form after prepositions or verbs, as, Between you and I, this is not easy to understand. He believed she and I to be against the plan. The animal next attacked John and I.

(c) Wrong case-form after *than* or *as*, as, He is three years older than me. You would rather talk with my brother than I.

It is to be noted that the forms of the verb *to be*, and of other verbs of being and becoming, take the *same case after as before*. The subject of an infinitive verb is put in the objective case. *Than* and *as* compare words that are in the same case, whether nominative or objective.

Exercise 126. Ungrammatical uses of pronouns.— *Correct the following, giving reasons:—*

1. If either the engineer or the fireman had lost their head one moment, there would have occurred a terrible accident. 2. No one can save their soul by good resolutions. 3. Whom did you think I was? 4. Who do you think I saw? 5. Who do you suppose him to be? 6. Who did you take him for? 7. Not a child should leave this room without putting on all the wraps they have brought. 8. Has any of you people lost their knife? 9. Mary can read as well as him. 10. The teacher, it seems to me, would sooner promote her than I. 11. Who can we tell about it? 12. This is a pretty position for you and I to be in. 13. Whom do you say was elected? 14. The thing for you and I to do, friends, is to change all this at once. 15. Who did you say he told to go?

5. *Verb with wrong number or tense.*—Perhaps the commonest example of disagreement of verb with subject in everyday speech is *he don't* (she don't, it don't) for *he doesn't*. Other examples of false agreement are in the following exercise. With regard to tense-forms, one should note particularly the fault of wrongly inserting *have* when the sense does not

require it. If you think of the intended meaning
you will see, for example, that " I expected to have
called yesterday," should be " I expected to call yesterday." It should be observed also that a statement true for all time is put in the present tense
even when the principal verb is in a past tense;
thus, " I said that air *is* a mixture of oxygen and
nitrogen."

Exercise 127. Verbs. — *Point out the false syntax in
the following sentences:* —

1. Each of those books, as Mr. Williams says, contain good
reading. 2. Neither of these pencils write well. 3. The
building with all its contents were destroyed by fire. 4. This
is not a color like scarlet or purple which tire the eyes.
5. Nothing but games and idle pursuits interest him any more.
6. Either this box or that one are worth buying at such a
price. 7. While the state of affairs are as I have described,
there suddenly appears on the scene a robber and his son, a
youth of eighteen. 8. Why is the smoking of cigars and the
drinking of beer allowed in this place? 9. Either you or I
are to stay, while Mary and you, or Mary and I, am to go.
10. If one of these chances are again presented, which happen
none too often, he or I is to start at once. 11. Our joy or our
sorrow are really due in large part to ourselves. 12. Neither
of those persons seem to be able to understand me. 13. How
high did you say the Washington monument was? 14. What
study was it you failed in? 15. The minister said that God
was no respecter of persons. 16. I never expected to have
been accused of insincerity. 17. I admit that I failed to
have proved that statement. 18. Hopkins had hoped to
have graduated this year. 19. I was not aware that this was
now your house. 20. I knew he wished to have advised me
not to have gone.

6. *Misplacing of adverbial modifiers.* — The infinitive verb and the particle " to " should not be separated by an adverbial or other element. The placing of adverbial modifiers with respect to the position of the verb is a subject requiring some attention. (See Maxwell's *Advanced Lessons in English Grammar*, article 597.) It should be particularly noted that, while an adverb may generally precede a simple verb, yet, when the verb is in a compound tense, the adverb usually comes after the first auxiliary if the verb is in the active voice, and next to the principal verb if it is in the passive voice.

Exercise 128. Misplaced modifiers.—*Rewrite the following sentences so as to avoid misplacing the adverbials. In correcting these sentences care must be taken not to put an unimportant word in an emphatic position.*

1. He determined to immediately ask the teacher's pardon. 2. We have concluded to not read it at present. 3. The weeks in his course of study were so arranged as to each in itself take up a certain part of the subject and complete it. 4. It is my wish to most completely repair the injury I have done them. 5. He intended to, if possible, return without being seen. 6. Agnes could hope now to only see her mother once again. 7. This writing is too bad to be easily read. 8. We shall have then been here ten days. 9. That game easily can be learned. 10. I have very rapidly walked home. 11. He read the book that I gave him with great care. 12. He will finish probably before dinner.

7. *Grammatical incompleteness.* — This is the fault of omitting a word required for the grammatical construction of a sentence. This fault nearly always

springs from carelessness, but it is very common, and the danger of falling into it should be understood.

A few examples are given, in the (attempted) sentences of the following exercise, which were actually written by school children. Other sentences illustrating grammatical incompleteness are to be found in Chapter VIII, on clearness, page 113.

Exercise 129. Grammatical incompleteness. — *Correct the following : —*

1. He was taking a step the consequences of which he was not quite sure. 2. Taking, for example, the Greeks at the beginning of their history were fond of hearing and repeating fables. 3. He made it a practice to experiment with all he came into contact. 4. If we take, for instance, a child coming late to school is made to stay after the others have gone home. 5. On the other hand if we could learn by the experience of others (as by reading and observing) and start our lives with this knowledge, as a child of to-day accepts the automobile, the steam engine, and the telephone without inquiring how these came to be. 6. You now pass from the condition you are in less time than it takes to tell it. 7. By charity I understand that not to give money always, but to give attention and sympathy when we find a chance.

II. *Skillful choice in diction.*

If the words given in pairs in Exercise 122, near the beginning of this chapter, are used wrongly, one for the other, it is simply a blunder due to ignorance. But there are in the English language many wordgroups, in each of which the meanings are so nearly the same that in many cases one of the words or expressions would be quite as *correct* as another. Is there any difference, for example, between *begin* and *commence?* But even among such words there is usually, for each particular case, a best word. We must, therefore, try to learn how to choose words with accuracy and good judgment. We learn to do this mainly by *much reading* of well-written books; in that way we gradually come to feel how certain words or kinds of words ought to be used. The English language, containing as it does words from many other tongues (see Appendix II), is so rich in words, that one might be· learning new uses or even new expressions all one's life.

Words having nearly the same meaning are called *synonyms.* In reality, as has been said, there is always a choice among synonyms. One word may be more agreeable in sound than any of its synonyms ; or more specific, or more emphatic. Sometimes synonyms differ in the degrees or intensities of the idea they express, as, grateful, pleasing, refreshing, delightful, intoxicating. It is in choosing among such words that care is especially needed. There are persons to whom everything they like, from soda water to scenery, is "lovely," or "elegant," or "so nice"; and to whom whatever they dislike is "horrid" or '· perfectly awful" or "fierce."

The usual reason, however, for distinctions among synonyms, is that the words have come, in the course of time, to be used most appropriately in certain connections. Thus, sincere, honest, genuine, real, all have an element of common meaning, yet each has its own proper use. Should one say genuine sympathy, or sincere sympathy; honest indignation or real indignation? Or, compare the words: old, aged, ancient, antiquated, venerable. Of these *old* has the widest range of use, but it implies a less amount of duration than *ancient; aged* is applied mostly to living beings; *venerable* suggests the admirable qualities of age, while *antiquated* means old fashioned, out of date, obsolete, of less value than formerly.

For the proper study of words each pupil should have a dictionary and a book containing lists of synonyms. There should also be in the schoolroom an unabridged dictionary, a large standard book on synonyms, and a copy of Roget's *Thesaurus of English Words.*

Exercise 130. Choice of words. — *Select adjectives of praise or commendation to be applied fitly to the following nouns:* —

Sunset, book, roast of beef, opinion, distinction, sentence, soup, apple, lady, essay, preacher, character, disposition, bouquet, vase, picnic, journey, hat, bonnet, party, weather, mountain, violin playing.

Exercise 131. Use of synonyms. — *Concerning the following words consult a dictionary, or a good book of synonyms. Select from each group, first, the word that has the widest use; then write a sentence containing it, and other sentences containing the other words of the group, so as to show the accurate use of each word.*

1. Gruff, ill natured, sullen, sour, surly, gloomy.
2. Glad, happy, jolly, joyful, pleased, blessed.

3. Warm, hearty, genial, cordial, ardent.
4. Close, sultry, stifling, suffocating, oppressive, stuffy.
5. Plentiful, abundant, adequate, sufficient, generous, lavish, ample.
6. Destroy, abolish, exterminate, obliterate, ruin, wipe out, annul.
7. Wrath, anger, rage, resentment, indignation, exasperation.
8. Try, attempt, endeavor, strive, undertake, essay.
9. Character, reputation, temper, temperament, disposition, constitution.
10. Charity, compassion, pity, mercy, kindness, goodwill, benevolence, benignity, sympathy.

Exercise 132. Synonyms.—*Make lists of four or more synonyms for each of the following words, and be ready to use each of your words accurately in a sentence:*—

1. Brave. 2. Convince. 3. Clear. 4. Injury. 5. Difficult. 6. Sorrow. 7. Gleam. 8. Answer. 9. Haughty. 10. Baffle.

Exercise 133. Choice of synonyms. — *In the following passages select from the words given in parentheses the word you think fittest for the place. In doing this consider the sound of the word as well as its accurate meaning.*

1. In a (moment, instant, second) all was again (silenced, still, hushed). Dead (noiselessness, silence, quiet, stillness) succeeded the (roar, bellow, growl, noise, reverberation) of the thunder, the (howl, roar, rush, noise) of the waters, the (groaning, howling, moaning, outcry, yelling) of the beasts, the (twittering, chattering, screaming, outcry) of the birds. Nothing was heard save the (dash, splash, plash, beating) of the (agitated, troubled, disturbed, roughened) lake, as it beat up against the black rocks which girt it in.

2. Not long since, a gentleman was (journeying, traveling) in one of the counties of Virginia, and about the close of the day stopped at a (hotel, inn, public house) to (get, have, obtain, procure) (supper, an evening meal, refreshment, food) and (spend, pass) the night. He had been there but a (little, short, inconsiderable) time, before an (aged, old, ancient) man alighted from his gig, with the (obvious, evident, apparent, seeming) (purpose, design, intention) of becoming his fellow guest at the same house.

3. Urge every (person, body, one) within reach of your influence to be always (neat, nice, trim, tidy, spruce) and (cleanly, clean, spotless), and give (them, him) means of being so. In so far as they (entirely, wholly, absolutely, positively) refuse, you must (abandon, leave off, give up, relinquish, cease) the effort, with (respect, regard) to them, only (seeing, looking out, taking care) that no children within your sphere of influence shall any more be (reared, raised, brought up) with such (customs, habits); and that every person who (is willing, consents, agrees, endeavors) to dress with (care, propriety) shall have (assistance, help, encouragement) to do so.

4. And, (indeed, in fact, in truth, to be sure, certainly,) if there were to be any (difference, distinction, unlikeness, dissimilarity) between a girl's education and a boy's, I (should, would) say that of the two the girl should be earlier (taken, introduced, led, started), as her (mind, intellect, brain, power of thought) ripens faster, into (profound, deep) and (grave, solemn, serious, great) subjects.

5. The (cliff, bluff, precipice) called "Starved Rock," now (shown, pointed out, indicated) to travelers as the (main, great, chief, most striking) natural (curiosity, formation) of the (region, district, section, vicinity, place,) (rises, ascends, stands up) (steep, sheer, abrupt) on three sides as a castle wall, to the height of a hundred and twenty-five feet above the (water, stream, river). In front, it overhangs the water that (laves, laps, washes) its (foot, base); its western (crest, summit, brow) looks down on the (tips, tops, heads) of the forest trees below,

and on the east (lies, extends, spreads, reaches out) a wide gorge, or ravine, (choked, stuffed, filled, piled) with the (mixed, mingled, various) foliage of oaks, walnuts, and elms; while in its (rugged, rough, stony, rocky, jagged) depths a little (stream, rivulet, brook, creek) creeps down to mingle with the river.

III. Suggestion in words. — Most words are mere matter-of-fact words, that is, they convey an idea without suggesting anything of pleasure or of displeasure connected with it. "Little valley" is about the same in meaning as "dell" or "dale," but the latter words are, by reason of their history or use, poetic, full of pleasant suggestion, while "little valley" is a plain and, as we say, colorless expression. Scientific books, and most school books, are written usually in plain, everyday English, for in them the object is merely clear explanation. But writing that is intended to give pleasure is full of color, warmth, imagination, suggestion, or, in one word, feeling.

We have already learned in studying description (Chapter V) how important it is to express the sense-impressions and the feelings that the thing or person described produces in us. We have also learned (in Chapter X) that specific words are more emphatic and lively than general words; this is because specific words usually suggest more than general words. Thus, "dale" is a particular kind of valley. The more general term suggests less. In the same way, when we see the word "plant," less is suggested to us, we see less and feel less, than when we see the word "rosebush."

In the following selections note the words that are printed in italics.   They are not plain, colorless, unsuggestive words, but they express some sort of feeling, either pleasurable or the opposite.

" And soon the *dappled softening* sky gave some earnest of its mood; for a brisk south wind arose, and the *blessed* rain came driving; *cold,* indeed, yet most *refreshing* to the skin, · all *parched* with snow, and the eyeballs so long *dazzled.*" — Blackmore, *Lorna Doone.*

" Here comes a big, *rough* dog, a countryman's dog in search of his master, smelling at everybody's heels, and *touching* little Annie's hand with his *cold* nose, but hurrying away, though she would *fain* have patted him. — Hawthorne, *Twice-Told Tales.*

" Let their last feeble and *lingering* glance rather behold the *gorgeous* ensign of the Republic, now known and *honored* throughout the earth, still full high advanced, its arms and trophies *streaming* in their original *luster,* not a stripe erased or *polluted,* not a single star *obscured.*" — Webster, Speech in Reply to Hayne.

" There is certainly some *chill* and *arid* knowledge to be found upon the *summits* of formal and *laborious* science; but it is all round about *you,* and for the *trouble* of looking, that you will acquire the *warm* and *palpitating* facts of life."— Stevenson, *Virginibus Puerisque.*

Suppose we try to put this last statement into plain and unsuggestive language.   It would become something like this, " There is certainly some merely intellectual knowledge to be found in the study of science; but everywhere and without study are to be acquired the facts of human life."

Exercise 134. Suggestive use of words. — *In the following groups, select the words that are suggestive, agreeably or disagreeably, and write sentences containing such words. State also which words are plain and matter-of-fact.*

1. Walked, limped, skipped, hobbled, moved, hurried.
2. Touch, caress, fondle, pet, handle, seize.
3. High, lofty, tall, commanding, noble, grand, stupendous, impressive.
4. Small, inconsiderable, petty, mean, contemptible, delicate, fine, minute, tiny.
5. Looked, gazed, stared, glared, glowered, observed, beamed.
6. Green, verdant, emerald, fresh, succulent, juicy.
7. Smell, sniff, odor, fragrance, aroma, stench.
8. Unlighted, dark, dismal, gloomy, darksome, dim, obscure, shady.
9. Large, extensive, vast, great, limitless, tremendous, enormous, immense, overwhelming.
10. Dry, waterless, arid, parched, moistureless, juiceless, sere.

Exercise 135. Suggestive use of adjectives. — *Such adjectives as the following were doubtless originally applied to objects known through the senses. But they can be applied, suggestively, to states of the mind or feelings, or to character or some abstract idea. Write sentences containing these adjectives so applied.*

1. Dull. 2. Keen. 3. Bright. 4. Narrow. 5. High.
6. Fine. 7. Hazy. 8. Sweet. 9. Hard. 10. White.
11. Black. 12. Solid. 13. Hollow. 14. Cold. 15. Lukewarm.

Exercise 136. Criticism of composition. — *Look over one or more of the letters recently written by you, and rewrite, substituting, wherever it is possible, more accurate or more suggestive words in place of those you have used.*

CHAPTER XIV

EXPOSITION AND ARGUMENT

WE have heretofore been mainly concerned with description and narration, as those are the commoner kinds of composition, and require less study or preparation of material than the kinds we are now to consider. Before we can write an exposition of a subject or enter into an argument, we ought to do either some reading or some thinking, and usually both.

I. *Exposition.* — The object in exposition is to explain a subject clearly, and as satisfactorily and fully as our space admits, or as suits our purpose. If possible, we ought also to make our treatment of the subject not dry and merely matter-of-fact, but somewhat interesting and entertaining. This may be done by a suggestive and pleasing choice of words, and by sprinkling a few ideas and observations amid the facts presented.

In preparing for an exposition, we need to get abundant information on the subject. This we may get in several ways : —

1. By thinking,   3. By conversations,
2. By observation,   4. By reading.

" But," you may ask, " how can one get information just by thinking over a subject ? " It may be
admitted that thinking does not of itself give us
information, but that we should think about our
subjects for exposition is so important that thinking
should be put first of all. We cannot know what
to look for in our reading unless we have thought
enough about the subject to have discovered certain
questions that need to be answered.

For expositions, since they aim at explaining a
subject, will have to answer for the reader all his
reasonable questions. In most expositions, these
questions are apt to be such as the following : —

1. What is the meaning or definition of the subject?
2. What kinds of it are there ?
3. Where does it come from ?
4. How is it made ? or how does it grow?
5. What are the parts of it ?
6. What are the uses of it ?
7. What are its effects or influences ?

In writing expositions we must carefully plan out
the composition in advance, making sure that what
we say shall have completeness and unity. If you
went to hear a lecture on " Cricket," and the speaker
should tell about the popularity of the game in England, the origin of it, and the way it was formerly
played, and then should praise it as a better game
than baseball, but should omit to explain how a
game of cricket is played, you would feel dissatis-

fied and think that the lecture lacked completeness, and that the talk about baseball could be spared, to the advantage of unity.

Exercise 137. Outlining for exposition. — *Without reading or talking on any of the following subjects, think out and write down for each one in the form of an outline the topics you think should be included in an exposition.*

1. The making of pottery.   2. The making of bricks. 3. Honey.   4. Yellow paint (ochre).   5. Olive oil.   6. Raisins.   7. Coffee.   8. Good roads.   9. Coal.   10. Gunpowder. 11. How to raise tomato plants.   12. Use of bicycles in war.   13. Bookbinding.   14. How thermometers are made. 15. Stamp collecting.   16. Cider.   17. Beer.   18. Maple syrup.   19. Weather forecasting.   20. Ants.

Exercise 138. Writing of expository paragraphs. — *On each of the following topics write a paragraph. Underscore the topic sentence.*

1. Danger of too little exercise, — effect on digestion — on the blood — on the circulation — on the brain.

2. Effects of a warm climate, — makes men lazy — much sleep — little brain work — no need of energetic work.

3. Learning to skate, — first efforts — difficulties — how to overcome them — cautions.

4. Disadvantages of large classes in school, — bad air — tendency to noise and inattention — teacher has too many to look after — each pupil receives less attention than in a small class.

5. Causes of the Spanish-American war, — the situation in Cuba — our commerce with Cuba — the feelings of the American people — the blowing up of the *Maine* — the political reasons.

Exercise 139. Writing of expositions. — *Prepare for a thorough and interesting exposition of one of the subjects given in Exercise 137, and make a complete outline. Write the composition, aiming at clearness and skillful choice of words. Avoid arguing; simply explain the subject. Later, write as many other expositions as the teacher may direct. There are some additional subjects given at the end of Chapter I.*

II. *Argument.* — In argument, the *subject*, if fully stated, must always be a *sentence*, because, for stating a truth or an untruth, a proposition is required. We must aim, in arguing, at clearness, but of course the main thing is *convincingness*. We wish, therefore, to get all the arguments we can that support our side of the question, and to weaken or overthrow all the arguments of our opponents.

There are several important matters to be kept in mind when we are preparing an argument : —

1. The subject must be clearly stated; and the meaning of it, and the words used in it, must be agreed upon, or made perfectly plain by definition. It is too common to see the opponents in debates argue about entirely different questions.

2. Do not waste time over unimportant matters; strike at the main points.

3. Remember that your opponent, real or imaginary, has arguments for his side of the question. You cannot ignore these. If you do, it will look as if you could not answer them. If you do not know what is to be said, or may be said, on the other side

of the question, you should devote some of your time to thinking and reading on that side. Answering your opponents' arguments is called *refutation*.

4. In writing or delivering your argument, it is well to adopt a courteous tone toward your adversary, and to be considerate and even complimentary toward your audience. Do not forget that you are trying, not only to convince the minds of the audience, but to persuade them to *feel* about the subject as you do.

The first great step in outlining or planning an argument is to divide the subject into two, three, or four main questions or aspects. Thus, if the subject is, —

Should women be granted the right to vote ?

you might consider the arguments under these heads : —

1. The justice of granting the suffrage to women.
2. The wisdom of it.

Or if the subject is, —

The sale of intoxicating liquors should be prohibited,

and you are on the negative or denying side, you might take for main divisions : —

1. Is prohibition desirable ?
2. Is it wise ?
3. Is it possible ? (or practicable ?)

Exercise 140. Division of argument. — *In a way similar to that just described, suggest main heads for the discussion of the following questions:* —

1. The spelling of English words should be reformed.
2. Hawthorne was a greater writer than Irving.
3. Examinations should be abolished.
4. Young persons should not read the newspapers.
5. French and German should not be taught in American schools.
6. Washington was not so great a man as Lincoln.
7. Writers are more useful than inventors.
8. Winter is to be preferred to summer.
9. The Spanish-American war should have been prevented.
10. Novel reading is a waste of time.
11. The observance of the Sabbath should be compulsory.
12. A man should always vote with his party.

We must in an argument try to get all the proofs we can. Proofs may be divided into three kinds or classes, the knowing of which will help us strengthen our argument : —

1. Proofs from what *might naturally be expected.*
2. Proofs from *observation* or *general knowledge.*
3. Proofs from the *experience* or the *opinions of others.*

All these may be (*a*) direct proofs, supporting our own side of the question, or (*b*) indirect proofs, weakening or overthrowing our opponents' side. Of the three classes of proofs just mentioned, the first is of course the least convincing. The second form of proof becomes more convincing in proportion to the carefulness of the observation recorded and the general acceptance of the knowledge stated. The third form of proof depends for its validity on the thorough-

ness with which evidence has been tested and the reputation and authority of the persons whose opinions
are quoted.

Exercise 141. Kinds of proofs. — *In the following
cases tell what kind of proof each one is:* —

(*a*) Subject, *A killed B.* 1. A was a man of bad and des-
perate character. 2. A blood-stained knife was found in his
room. 3. The effort to show that A staid at home on the
night of the murder fails. 4. He had been known as an
enemy of B. 5. After the murder, A was observed to have
more money to spend than before.

(*b*) Subject, *Is the United States as great a nation as England?*
1. The purpose of our forefathers was to secure and establish
freedom. 2. The territorial growth of the United States and
its increase in wealth and population. 3. The noble history
of England. 4. Unjustly privileged land-holding classes in
England. 5. The thousands of the poor and degraded in
London. 6. The alleged greater purity of English politics.
7. The negro population in America. 8. England's great
colonies. 9. Lincoln's opinion of the American government.
10. Dickens's opinion (in *American Notes*). 11. Lawless
regions in the United States.

When we have undertaken an argument, we should,
after stating our main divisions of the whole, set to
work to think out, or else get from reading, proofs
of all the three classes above named, including those
supporting our side and those against the other side.
All these proofs should be arranged under the main
heads, and there we have our outline, or, as it is often
called in argumentation, our *brief.* For example : —

Brief on the subject, *Composition is a more important study than arithmetic :* —

I. Introduction

    (*a*) Meaning of composition and arithmetic

    (*b*) Meaning of " important "

    (*c*) Division of subject (see *a* and *b* under discussion)

II. Discussion

    (*a*) Composition is more important *in school* than arithmetic is.

        1. Writing is necessary in most other school studies.

        2. Oral recitation, which is a form of composition, is necessary in all school studies.

        3. Composition work trains us how to think and reason; this is valuable for all school work.

        4. Arithmetic is mostly a matter of memory and practice.

        5. Composition work leads us to understand, consider, and appreciate all we read in school.

    (*b*) Composition is more important *out of school* than arithmetic is.

        1. It is natural to expect this, because in life we do so much more reading and writing than figuring.

2. To be able to write well is important in more occupations than to be able to compute.

3. All but the simpler kinds of arithmetical work are never used after one leaves school.

4. There is a great demand from business men for assistants who can write good English.

5. In later life it is important to be able to win people to one's ideas by writing or talking well.

6. We may derive much pleasure from good writing and the appreciation of good reading.

7.' The opinion of . . . and . . . on this question.

III. Conclusion

(a) Summing up of the arguments
(b) Statement of the conclusion

Exercise 142. Preparation of brief. — *Following more or less the plan just given, prepare a full outline or brief on one side of one of the subjects given in Exercise 140 or at the end of Chapter I.*

Exercise 143. Written argument. — *From the brief called for in Exercise 142, or from a brief on some other question than the one formerly selected, write out the argument in full, in the form of a speech. In doing this, bear in mind what is said on page 211, about how to make arguments strong. If you quote* *opinions, let them be those of persons regarded as authorities; if you offer as facts statements not of your own knowledge, try to ascertain, and to convince your readers or hearers, that the statements are true.*

Exercise 144. Criticism. — *After completing the argument called for in the last exercise, criticise it, sentence by sentence, with regard to clearness, unity, and paragraphing.*

1. Any superfluous "ands"?
2. Any sentence containing unconnected ideas?
3. Any faulty use of pronouns?
4. Any misplacing of modifiers?
5. Any paragraphs without definite topic and unity?

Exercise 145. Criticism. — *Now read critically the essay again, this time with respect to emphasis and choice of words.*

1. Any opportunity for interrogation, exclamation, or direct quotation?
2. Any need of repetition of a word, or any place for cutting out unnecessary words?
3. Any opportunity to change to order of climax or of periodic sentence?
4. Any chance to introduce simile or metaphor?
5. Any possible improvement in choice of words, so as to use more accurate, specific, emphatic, or suggestive terms?

Exercise 146. Oral debate. — *Let the class choose sides on some question for debate, then let each member of the class collect arguments for his side and arrange them in a brief. Let the class on the appointed day form itself into a debating society, elect a president and a secretary, and debate the question, all speaking in turn. The teacher is to decide which side wins.*

APPENDIX I

MARKS FOR USE IN CRITICISM OF COMPOSITIONS

NOTE.—Some of these marks relate to general faults, and some to very specific ones. The teacher will, of course, use such of the marks as he believes most suitable, and will add others if the need for them appears.

Both the outline and the composition should be criticised.

To show that a marginal criticism refers to some special word or words, the latter may be underlined or marked out or inclosed in brackets. It is often well to let the pupil find out for himself what word in the line is, for example, misspelled.

Two or more of the marks may be combined, as, O inc, outline incomplete ; U ns, lack of unity, divide into shorter sentences.

ab   Abrupt; lack of introductory words, or sudden change of subject without making connection.

ad   Adjective wrongly used for adverb, or adverb for adjective. (After verbs of being, or becoming, or seeming, the adjective is correct, as it describes the subject and does not limit the verb; as, She is looking beautiful to-night.)

agr   Agreement faulty, either of verb and subject, or of pronoun and antecedent.

amb   Ambiguous; word or expression may be understood in two ways. (As, We saw certain signs of a storm. Here *certain* may mean some, or sure, unmistakable.)

arr   Arrangement faulty, causing either lack of *clearness* or lack of *emphasis* (as by climax or suspended construction; see Chapter X, on emphasis).

c   Capital required, or capital wrongly used (see Appendix III).

ch   Choice of word poor; word not accurately used, or weak (trite, too general, or unsuggestive; see Chapter XIII).

cl   Lack of clearness; from faulty use of pronoun, from faulty arrangement, from omission of necessary word or words, or from confusion of ideas.

cond   Condense; cut out unnecessary words, phrases, or even sentences.

conn   Connective ill chosen; avoid the "and" habit; study the table of conjunctions, page 85.

cons   Improper change of construction; in using contrasting or added clauses or phrases, seek to make the expressions similar (see page 151).

cxs   Combine or recast into a complex sentence.

d   Diction faulty; no such word, consult the dictionary.

eu   Lack of euphony; combination of words disagreeable to the ear.

excl   Transform the sentence into the exclamatory form, or back into the declarative.

F   Lack of force, due to weak arrangement or poor choice of expression.

gr n   Bad grammar, disagreement in number.

gr t   Bad grammar, wrong tense of verb used.

inc   Incomplete; necessary part of sentence, or of entire composition, or of outline, omitted.

intrg   Recast the sentence into the interrogatory form, or back into the declarative.

mar   Margin not properly looked after.

mis   Misstatement of fact.

N   Lack of neatness.

ns   Put a period, and begin a new sentence.

p   Bad punctuation. Study the rules for punctuation given in Appendix III.

pl   Use the plural, or change to the singular.

pos   Position wrong; word too far removed from its modifier; or word misplaced that should be in emphatic position, that is, at the beginning or at the end of the sentence.

poss Use the possessive case; spell it correctly (see Appendix III for rules for writing the possessive case of nouns, page 239).

O Outline faulty, disorderly, incomplete, or badly arranged.

onf Outline not followed in the composition. The topics of the outline should be taken up in their proper order, and the composition paragraphed according to the plan of the outline.

om Omission of necessary word or words. In the writing opposite this mark the teacher or critic may place a caret ($\wedge$) where the omission has occurred.

quot Use direct quotation for emphasis, and punctuate the sentence accordingly (see Appendix III, page 236).

red Redundancy; use of superfluous words or repetition of idea.

ref Reference not clear. This may be true of a pronoun, a participle, an adjective, or any other modifier.

re b Repetition bad; find synonym or change the expression.

re g Repetition good; repeat word or expression for clearness or emphasis.

rel Relative pronoun wrongly chosen; restrictive for coördinative, or the reverse, or change of pronoun required by euphony (see page 190).

rew Rewrite; recast the sentence, or rewrite the entire composition, according to the position of the mark.

S Bad spelling.

sim Use a simile or a metaphor to explain or emphasize your idea.

sms Use simple sentence; recast, condense, or combine into a simple sentence.

subd Subdivide the topic; give the points it includes.

t Topic of this paragraph not clear. Make it so; introduce, if necessary, a topic sentence.

tr Transpose.

U   Unity violated. Sentence contains unrelated ideas or too many ideas; or paragraph does not have unity.

¶   Paragraph. See outline or observe change of topic.

ɴo ¶   Do not paragraph; topic has not changed.

∽   Transpose. (Mark to be used in the body of the text, not in the margin.)

∧   Some letter, word, or words omitted here; or else a separation into two words is necessary. (Mark to be used in the body of the text, not in the margin.)

δ   Strike out or omit.

(-)   Hyphen lacking or word wrongly divided.

⊙   Period omitted.

X   Error.

?   Probable error.

∕ or ∖   Calls attention to a letter or to a place for punctuation. (Mark to be used in the body of the text, not in the margin.)

APPENDIX II

ENGLISH WORDS

NOTE. — In connection with sections I and II of this Appendix may be read the Historical Sketch of the English Language given in Maxwell's *Advanced Lessons in English Grammar*, pp. 314–322.

I. *Sources of English words.* — There are three main elements in the English vocabulary: the Saxon, the French, and the Latin. The French itself is largely of Latin origin. The mingling of the Saxon and the French elements, five to six hundred years ago, formed the English language. Many words since then have been added from the Latin and the Greek and from most of the modern languages.

The original inhabitants of England were Celts, called Britons. From about 100 A.D. to 400 A.D. they were subject to Rome. The Roman soldiers withdrew in 410 A.D. Very few modern English words are derived either from the Celtic or from the Latin of those times.

The Saxons came from Germany, and conquered and settled England during the fifth century A.D. (beginning in the year 449).

Six centuries later, in the year 1066, the Norman French, under William the Conqueror, invaded England and subjugated the Saxons. Thereafter, for about three hundred years, there were two distinct languages spoken in England, — the Saxon, mostly by the humbler classes and the serfs; the French, by the Normans. *Chaucer*, the author of the *Canterbury Tales*, was the first great writer in the English or mixed tongue (1340–1400). His English is not so much unlike ours of to-day but that it can be read with very little trouble.

When and how did the Latin contributions come in? Easily and frequently. There were many monks and churchmen in England from early Saxon times on. All these read and spoke Latin. Later, in the times following the period when Chaucer lived, there were many scholars and learned men who wrote Latin, although English was their native tongue. When such men wrote English, they naturally introduced many Latin words in an "Englished" form. Examples of this late Latin contribution (fifteenth century) may be taken from this and the preceding paragraph: century, invaded, subjugated, distinct, author, contributions, frequently, period (originally from Greek), naturally, introduced, preceding, paragraph (originally from Greek). Note that these words are rather long. If you consult a dictionary, you will see how very like they are to the Latin (or Greek) words from which they are derived.

The following examples of words of French extraction are found in the same two paragraphs. (Note that these words are a good deal changed from the

Latin originals. Some French words are not of Latin, but of Germanic or of Celtic origin.)

language (Fr. *langage*, from *langue*, from L. *lingua*, a tongue).
class (Fr. *classe*, from L. *classis*, an assembly, a fleet).
serf (Fr. from L. *servus*, a slave, from *servio*, serve).
humble (Fr. from L. *humilis*, lowly, from *humus*, the ground).
very (Old Fr. *verai*, *vray*, from supposed Low Latin *veracus*, from L. *verax*, *veracis*, meaning veracious, truthful).
trouble (Fr. from L. *turbula*, a little crowd, a disorderly crowd, from *turba*, a crowd).
example (Fr. from L. *exemplum*, a specimen, from *eximo*, pick out, buy).

The word "monk," which was used in the same paragraph, is from Latin *monachus* (original Greek meaning, living alone, solitary). This word, as an English word, goes back to the earliest days of the Roman church in England. The form of it in Anglo-Saxon was *munec* or *munuc*. The word "scholar" is from Saxon *scōlere*, from *scōlu*, a school, but this came from Latin *schola*, a school (originally Greek). The h in scholar was introduced much later, to make the word agree with Latin *scholaris*, pertaining to a school.

Practically, all the other words in those two paragraphs are of Saxon origin.

If we liken the history of the English language to the course of a river, we should imagine the stream of original Saxon words flowing on with but little change from the time of the Saxon conquest (fifth century) to the time of its junction with the Norman French language (fourteenth century). During those nine long centuries the Saxon speech accepted a few words from the conquered Britons (whose descendants live now mostly in Wales, Ireland, and upper Scotland); a few from the Danes (who invaded England repeatedly in the ninth and tenth centuries, and finally set Danish kings for a time on the Saxon throne); and a few words of Latin or Greek origin from the monks and priests (the words "monk," "priest" and "scholar" are examples of this class). The Saxon also lost many of its word-endings or inflections. In the early Saxon there were over fifteen case-forms of the article "the."

After the great junction of Saxon and French, five to six hundred years ago, the enlarged stream, now English, received, in the fifteenth and sixteenth centuries, many words from the Latin and not a few from the Greek. As the English people spread over the globe, they encountered many languages and adopted many words.

Thus, from the American Indian we have wigwam, papoose, squaw, canoe, and the like. So we have from the Spanish such words as alligator, potato, negro, cork, cigar, tornado, and vanilla; from the Italian many words, such as balcony, cameo, cartoon, soprano, piano, macaroni, pistol, and umbrella. From French we have blonde, bouquet, bivouac, trousseau; from German, nickel, meerschaum, quartz; from Hebrew, abbey, cherub, Sabbath; from Arabic, alcohol, algebra, zero, gazelle, lute; and so on from many other languages.

The histories of the following words are peculiar and interesting, worth copying into your notebook: calico, copper, dollar, check, gypsy, tantalize, assassin, panic, sincere, tariff, salary, silly, slave, vandalism, daisy, dahlia, galvanic, Friday, July, January. Many other words of curious history will be found explained, usually with correctness, in Trench's *On the Study of Words.*

Finally, in recent times, down to the present, as new discoveries and inventions have been made, and new sciences developed, many words have been coined, mostly for scientific or technical use, and chiefly from Latin and Greek. Examples of such words are biology, geology, phonograph, telephone, telegraph, photograph, photosphere, spectroscope, electrolysis.

II. *Description of the classes of English words.* — Counting English words as they are listed in a dictionary, those of Saxon origin are a much less number than those from the Latin. But the Saxon or native English words are used, in ordinary writing or speech, far more than the words of Latin origin. They nearly always outnumber the latter, if we group according to origin the words used on a page in a book, because the Saxon words are used over and over. We can easily write whole pages without using a word of Latin origin, but we could hardly write one sentence without using words of Saxon origin.

The Saxon element in English includes, generally speaking : —

1. All the pronouns.

2. All the prepositions.

3. All the conjunctions.

4. All the numeral adjectives, except *second*, and the articles.

5. All the auxiliary verbs.

·6· Most of the nouns, adjectives, verbs, and adverbs expressing simple everyday ideas.

Words of French and Latin origin are usually more general and abstract. Compare the following: —

Words of Saxon origin	From French or Latin
walk, go, run, skip, hop, jump, leap, fly, swim, crawl,	move, proceed,
eye, nose, ear, hand, tongue, cheek, foot, head,	feature, part,
red, yellow, green, blue, brown, black, white,	tint, color,
father, mother, brother, sister, son, daughter,	parent, relative,
fox, bird, fowl, snake, whale, bee, cat, hound, wolf.	beast, creature, animal.

Perhaps the simplest way to compare the French and the Latin elements in English is to place side by side, in pairs, English words: (1) from the Norman French, adopted mostly in the fourteenth century; (2) from the Latin direct, coming in later than the fourteenth century — mostly book-words at first, only gradually adopted into speech.

(1) From the French	(2) From the Latin	(3) The Latin words
benison	benediction	benedictionem
sir, sire	senior	seniorem
feat	fact	factum
chance	cadence	cadentiam
loyal	legal	legalem
royal, real	regal	regalem
poor	pauper	pauperem

poison	potion	potionem
caitiff	captive	captivum
sure	secure	securum
treason	tradition	traditionem
frail	fragile	fragilem
parcel	particle	particulam
sever	separate	separatum

If it seems hard to understand how the words in the first column came from those in the third, we must remember that for centuries there existed no written French or English, and that until after the invention of printing in the fifteenth century, there were so few books that languages were preserved only by custom in speech. Spoken languages naturally change from period to period. Words are usually worn down and shortened in common speech, as may be seen from the table just given.

III. *Word-formation.*

In Maxwell's *Advanced Lessons in English Grammar*, Part II, Chapter IV, pp. 206–221, there is to be found a much fuller treatment of the subject of word-formation in English than can or need be given here. There are also given exercises.

The following are short lists of *prefixes and suffixes* of English words: —

ENGLISH PREFIXES

for-, fore-, mis-, un-, be-, with-, en-.

LATIN PREFIXES

ab-, ad-, ante-, bi-, contra-, cum- (French col-, com-, coun-, cor-), di-, in-, ex-, per-, pre-, pro-, post-, se-, semi-, sub-, super-, trans-.

GREEK PREFIXES

anti-, auto-, dia-, epi-, hemi-, mono-, peri-, syn-.

ENGLISH SUFFIXES	LATIN SUFFIXES	GREEK SUF-FIXES
For nouns:	*For nouns:*	*For nouns:*
-dom, -hood, -ing, -ness, -ship, -ie, -ling, -ster, -ard.	-age, -ance, -ence, -ion, -ment, -tude, -ty, -y, -or, -ary, -er, -ate, -ist.	-sis.
For adjectives:	*For adjectives :*	*For adjectives:*
-ed, -ern, -en, -fold, -ful, -ish, -less, -ly, -some, -wise, -ward.	-acious, -al, -ant, -able, -ar, -ent, -ible, -ic, -id, -il, -ive, -lent, -ose (-ous), -und.	-ic.
For verbs:	*For verbs:*	*For verbs:*
-en.	-ate, -fy.	-ize (-ise).

The following are some of the most useful Latin and Greek *root-words* employed in English word-formation. (pp. stands for past participle, as *ard-*, burn, pp. *arsus*, burnt.)

Latin root-words, (*a*) verbs

ag-, do (pp. *actus*)
am-, love
aud-, hear
cap-, take (pp. *captus*)
cad-, fall (pp. *casus*)
cred-, believe
ced-, go, come
dic-, say
doc-, teach
duc-, lead
fac-, make; **fi-,** become
leg-, read
mitt-, send (pp. *missus*)
nasc-, be born (pp. *natus*)

(*b*) nouns and adjectives

ager, field
anima, soul
animus, mind
annus, year
aqua, water
caput, head
carn-, flesh
cura, care
deus, god
finis, end
gradus, step
gravis, heavy
homo, man
littera, letter

pet-, seek
port-, carry
reg-, rule
stru-, build (pp. *structus*)
tang-, touch (pp. *tactus*)
sci-, know
scrib-, write (pp. *scriptus*)
spir-, breathe
terr-, frighten
vid-, see
vor-, eat, devour

m, great
manus, hand
mors, death
multus, many
novus, new
nox, night
omnis, all
ped-, foot
rota, wheel
terra, land
unus, one

Greek root-words

anthropos, man
bios, life
deka, ten
dunamis, power
ge, earth
graphein, write (*gramma*, something written)
hekaton, a hundred
hippos, horse
kuklos, circle
logos, speech, treatise
metron, measure
monos, alone

opsis, sight (*optikos*, pertaining to the sight)
orthos, right
petra, rock
phemi, speak
philein, love
phone, sound
skopein, see
sophia, wisdom
sphaira, globe
tele, distant, far
theos, god
tupos, a type, a figure

Properly coined words should combine Greek affixes with Greek words, Latin with Latin, and English with English. Such words as walkist, electrocution (from Gk. *electron*, amber, and the termination of the Latin word *executionem*, from *ex* and *sequor*, pp. *secutum*, follow), shadowgraph, burglarize, and cablegram, are badly coined.

IV. *Style as affected by the derivation of words.* — In each of the following two selections, both taken from Irving's *Stratford on Avon*, in the *Sketch-Book*, count up the number of words you take to be of Saxon origin and those of classical origin. In which selection is used the larger proportion of native English words? Which is the simpler style of writing? What in the character of the subject-matter made it natural for Irving to use more Saxon words in one passage than in the other?

Its situation is quiet and retired: the river runs murmuring at the foot of the churchyard, and the elms which grow upon its banks droop their branches into its clear bosom. An avenue of limes, the boughs of which are curiously interlaced, so as to form in summer an arched way of foliage, leads up from the gate of the yard to the church porch. The graves are overgrown with grass; the gray tombstones, some of them nearly sunk into the earth, are half covered with moss, which has likewise tinted the reverend old building. Small birds have built their nests among the cornices and fissures of the walls, and keep up a continual flutter and chirping; and rooks are sailing and cawing about its lofty gray spire.

As I crossed the bridge over the Avon on my return, I paused to contemplate the distant church in which the poet lies buried, and could not but exult in the malediction which has kept his ashes undisturbed in its quiet and hallowed vaults. What honor could his name have derived from being mingled in dusty companionship with the epitaphs and escutcheons and venal eulogiums of a titled multitude? What would a crowded corner in Westminster Abbey have been, compared with this reverend pile, which seems to stand in beautiful loneliness as his sole mausoleum! The solicitude about the grave may be but the offspring of an overwrought sensibility;

but human nature is made up of foibles and prejudices; and its best and tenderest affections are mingled with these factitious feelings.

The words italicized in the following selection (from Irving's *Westminster Abbey*) are of Latin or classical origin. Note the fine effect they produce by being placed in contrast with the simple and homely Saxon words.

The time must come when its gilded *vaults*, which now spring so loftily, shall lie in rubbish beneath the feet; when, instead of the sound of *melody* and *praise*, the wind shall whistle through the broken arches, and the owl hoot from the shattered tower — when the garish sunbeam shall break into these gloomy *mansions* of death; and the ivy twine round the fallen *column ;* and the foxglove hang its blossoms about the nameless *urn*, as if in mockery of the dead. Thus man passes away; his name *perishes* from *record* and *recollection;* his *history* is as a tale that is told, and his very *monument* becomes a *ruin*.

APPENDIX III

RULES FOR PUNCTUATION, CAPITALIZATION, AND SPELLING

Note. — These rules are adapted and condensed from Maxwell's *Advanced Lessons in English Grammar*, pp. 270–278 (punctuation); pp. 69–75 (rules for use of capitals and for spelling).

I. *Punctuation.*

Punctuation is necessary to mark (1) the close of a sentence; (2) pauses required in reading; (3) the elements or parts of sentences to be joined in meaning. It is a mistake to think punctuation of little importance. Accurate punctuation shows accurate thinking, an understanding of the construction of the sentence, and of the relations of the parts. You cannot punctuate correctly unless you think clearly and understand what you wish to say.

(*a*) The points used to mark the completion of a sentence are the period (.), the question mark (?), and the exclamation mark (!).

The *period* marks the *end* of every declarative and every imperative sentence, unless the words are spoken with strong feeling; then the exclamation mark is used; as, Go at once!

The *period* is also used to mark *abbreviations;* as, The Rev. John Sinclair, D.D., read from Rev. xxi.

The *question mark* is used after an interrogative sentence, and after a direct question contained in any sentence; example of the latter: When he asked "What are you going to do about it?" we made no reply.

The *exclamation mark* is used after declarative and imperative sentences expressing strong feeling, commonly after interjections, and after the nominative of address when strong feeling is to be indicated; as, John! John! What a mess you have made! Oh dear! What shall I do?

Never place together a question mark and a period, or an exclamation mark and a period. Use one or the other.

Exercise 147. Terminal punctuation. — *Put proper marks at the ends of the following sentences:* —

1. Breaking through that white streak of water near the shore comes a dark something, which soon takes form and is seen to be a steamer What a variety of craft haunt the lake The largest are these tall steamers, taller still for their red stacks At night, with their colored lights, they look like jeweled slippers

2. Let us think over this passage and examine its words First, is it not singular to find Milton assigning to St. Peter not only his full episcopal function, but the very types of it which Protestants usually refuse most passionately His "mitred" locks Milton was no bishop lover; how comes St. Peter to be "mitred"

(*b*) The points used within a sentence are the comma (,), the semicolon (;), the colon (:), the dash (—); quotation marks (" "), the parentheses [( )].

The *comma* is used : —

1. To separate the *nominative of address* from the rest of the sentence; as, O Cassius, thou art yoked with a lamb.

2. To mark the *beginning of a direct quotation* (but see also the rules for the use of the colon); as, The judge said, " Gentlemen of the jury, what is your verdict ? " If the quotation is not a question, and precedes the clause on which it depends, it is followed by a comma; as, " We are unable to agree," answered the foreman. If the clause on which a quotation depends is inserted between parts of the quotation, it is cut off by two commas; as, " We have," said the foreman, " been unable to agree; but, if your Honor will let us have a little more time, we may be able to reach a conclusion."

3. To separate a very *long subject* from its verb; as, Whatever you may wish to do about this matter of answering his letter, will be agreeable to me. Here the subject is the whole clause, and not *letter* or *answering*, as might be carelessly supposed. In general, however, *a single comma is not to be used between the subject and the verb*.

4. To cut off, at its beginning and at its end, a *parenthetical* or explanatory expression. This includes : —

Thrown-in words, like *however, to be brief, finally, besides, indeed, in fact, moreover.*

Nouns in apposition, especially when they are accompanied by modifiers; as, John Brown, the leader of the attack, was executed.

Relative clauses, when they are not restrictive but coördinate; as, John Brown, who led the attack, was executed.

Adjective and adverbial elements when they are inserted for explanation; as, General Wolfe, wounded and dying, learned of his great victory. That story is, in several particulars, improbable.

Adverbial clauses, when inserted for explanation; as, He determined that, if the chance were given him, he would set out for the Philippines at once.

5. To separate words in *series*, conjunctions being omitted; as, Poetry, music, painting, and sculpture are not the only fine arts. He was tall, broad-shouldered, muscular, and active.

6. To separate words in *pairs*, for the same reason; as, The flower and the star, the pebble and the mountain, the raindrop and the sea, all are the work of His hand.

7. To separate *clauses in a compound sentence*, when they are related in meaning; as, The rivulet becomes a brook, and the brook becomes a creek, and the creek becomes a river.

The *parentheses* are used to inclose a remark that might be omitted without destroying the sense of the sentence; as, Know then this truth (enough for man to know), virtue alone is happiness below.

It is a fault to make use of long parentheses. They interrupt and often obscure the sense.

The *quotation marks* are used : —

1. To inclose direct quotations. If a quotation includes another, the latter is inclosed in single inverted commas, to distinguish it from the main quotation, which is inclosed in the double inverted commas ; as, " Aha!" said my lord, " I go on the principle that ' a bird in the hand is worth two in the bush.' "

2. Sometimes to indicate titles of books, and nicknames.

The *dash* is used : —

1. To mark an abrupt turn in a sentence ; as, I will tell you — but no! why should I not keep my own counsel ?

2. To mark a significant pause that should be made in reading ; as, Now you listen to what I have to say — I will never give you what you demand !

3. To mark words in apposition, or other parenthetical expressions ; as, This work was performed four hundred years ago, and — such is the merit of good work — it endures to this day.

As a rule, it is better usage to set off parenthetical expressions by commas, than to set them off by dashes or parentheses.

Exercise 148. Punctuation. — *Which of the above rules for the use of commas, etc., are illustrated in the following sentences?*

1. There were the first editions of the immortal " Elia," he who had the "delightful art of making a delightful summer out of a single swallow."

2. Shakspere's town library has now every volume except *The Merchant of Venice*, which was, for some reason, never purchased.

3. Why should we judge him by his words, when all his works are there — a whole collection of them, by the by, is now being exhibited in Boston — to prove his power ?

4. The studio — a bare barn of a place, outside the Porta del Popolo — stood on a slope commanding a view of the monastery in which Luther, they say, dwelt, when he was planning his defiance of the Church.

5. The food was bad, the meal ill served, the landlord (heaven bless him!) was dirty, but what a talk we had about work, play, books, art, life!

Exercise 149. **Punctuation.** — *Punctuate, according to the rules for the use of the comma, etc., the following sentences:* —

1. Vedder said What do you think I have been studying lately fungi I showed an Italian friend some drawings which I had made from some specimens Why bless my soul said he you are going into this fungus line quite seriously are you not

2. Now having known him a good many years I realized what this task involved

3. Well I met a sort of second cousin there Alice Brooks I've known her since we were children

4. The ashes sighed he of my fondest hopes

5. Ah Mr Lever he said very blandly I didn't know you were in England in fact I was not even aware of your having asked for leave

The *semicolon* is the most commonly used stop, if we except the comma and the period.. The semicolon is, in general, used when the comma would not indicate so distinct a pause or so definite a division as is desired. If several coördinate clauses, for example, follow one another, and each or any of them contains commas for minor pauses, the semicolon must be used to separate such clauses; as, "Still more surprised were they to learn that, in order to have bread, wheat had to be sown in the ground; that grass was necessary for the production of milk; and that wine did not flow out of casks on a turning of a key." Examples of another use of the semicolon are to be found throughout this Appendix, before the word "as", when this is followed·by a sentence given for illustration.

The *colon* is used most commonly as follows : —

1. To indicate that a list, enumeration, or statement is to follow; as, "The following are the principal rules for punctuating the possessive case : First," etc. Under this rule comes the use of a colon before a direct quotation, when the quotation is to be marked as especially emphatic; as, The dealer then uttered these words: "I believe you have been trying to cheat me. I refuse to deal with you at all."

2. In a long complex or compound sentence, after groups of clauses, or sometimes phrases, when the members of the groups are separated by semicolons; as, If the man walked slowly, the lion lessened his pace; if the man stopped, the beast did likewise: but in spite of this seeming imitation of the man's movements, the lion was gradually gaining.

(*c*) Miscellaneous marks.

(1) The *apostrophe* (') is used to mark the omission of a letter when the abbreviated word is to be pronounced as it is spelled; as, don't, o'clock, o'er.

The apostrophe is a necessary part of all *nouns in the possessive case*, singular or plural. The rules for writing the possessive case are as follows:—

1. Nouns in the singular number add '*s* to the nominative form, whether the nominative ends in *s* or not; as, the man's, Charles's, Dickens's, Mr. Jones's, mouse's.

2. In the plural, if the nominative plural does not end in *s* or the sound of *s*, the apostrophe and *s* are added; as, men's, children's.

But if, as is usual, the plural already ends in *s*. only the apostrophe is added; as, girls' hats, the Joneses' house.

In short, to form the possessive, always add '*s*, except in the plural when the nominative plural ends in *s*.

In certain expressions, as, for goodness' sake, for conscience' sake, the *s* is omitted because there are already two *s* sounds present.

The pronouns *ours, hers, yours, its, theirs,* are written without any apostrophe.

(2) The *hyphen* (-) is used to connect the parts of a compound word, as, cathedral-tower; also to separate a word into its syllables. This usually is necessary only at the end of a line where there is room for only a part of a word. A word of one syllable should

never be written part on one line and part on the next. Words of more than one syllable should always be divided between syllables. For instance, to write alw-ays, or believ-ed, is wrong. In general, divide words so that the part beginning the next line shall begin with a consonant; as, re-quired, enumera-tion (not -ation). However, to divide before the syllable -ing, when it is preceded by a single conso-nant, is proper; as, follow-ing, eat-ing.

(3) The *caret* ($\wedge$) is used to mark an error of omis-sion in one's writing. It has been called the " blunder mark."

(4) Marks like * † ‡ § and others are used to direct attention to a note in the margin or elsewhere.

(5) *Underscoring* a word once indicates that it should be printed in italics; twice, in small capitals; three times or more, in large capitals, as for headings or title pages.

II. *Use of capital letters.*

Begin with capitals : —

1. The first word of every sentence, and of every line of poetry.

2. Every proper noun, every proper adjective (as French, Latin), every personified common noun (as, Then Peace shall smile upon us).

3. Every name or title of the Deity, pronouns pertaining to the Deity (this rule is to be followed with judgment; sometimes the repeated use of capi-

talized pronouns becomes tiresome and annoying), and names of religious denominations.

4. The names of the days of the week, the months of the year (but not the four seasons of the year, except when personified), and the four points of the compass when they denote great regions or sections of a country; as, He journeyed west and north till he had traversed the region called the great Northwest.

5. The important words in the title of a book or of an essay or of a poem.

6. Titles of honor or respect; as, The Honorable Member from Ohio; the Duke of Westminster; His Excellency, the Governor of North Carolina; His Honor, the Mayor.

7. Words to be particularly emphasized, such as words denoting an important epoch of history; as, The period of the Thirty Years' War.

8. The first word of a direct quotation, except when only a word, a phrase, or a clause is quoted and made a part of the writer's own sentence.

9. Write with capitals the pronoun I and the interjections O, Oh.

III. *Rules for spelling.*

1. Final *e* silent is generally omitted before a *suffix beginning with a vowel;* as, write, writ-ing; please, pleas-ing, pleas-ure; grieve, griev-ance; combine, combining; change, changing; slice, slicing. But since *c* and *g* have the "hard" sound before *a*, *o*, and *u*, the endings *ce* and *ge* must be retained

before suffixes ending in *a, o, u.* Thus, courageous, serviceable, changeable. The word singeing retains the *e* to distinguish it from singing; dyeing to distinguish it from dying. Shoeing and agreeable would be apt to be mispronounced if spelt shoing and agreable.

2. Final *e* is generally *retained* before a *suffix beginning with a consonant;* as, pale, paleness; dole, doleful. (Exceptions to this rule are judgment, acknowledgment, wholly, truly, and nursling.)

3. Words ending in a *single* consonant (preceded by a single vowel) *double* the final letter on taking a suffix beginning with a vowel, if the words are *monosyllabic* or *accented on the last syllable.* Thus, begiń, begińning; sit, sitting; underpinning, repellent, befitting. But if the words are accented on some other than the last syllable, or if the consonant is preceded by two vowels, the consonant is not doubled; as, trav'el-er, viv'id-est, of'fer-ing, wor'ship-er, prof'it-ing, fo'cusing, bi'as-ed; retaining, toiling, revealing.

4. Words ending in a *double consonant* usually retain it when *suffixes* are added; as, ebb, ebbing; will, willful; shrill, shrillness. (But note the exceptions, — almost, altogether, also, although, fulfill, belfry, welfare.)

5. Words ending in a double consonant usually retain it when *prefixes* are added; as, farewell, downfall, respell, undersell. (Note the exceptions, — until, and adjectives ending in *-ful.*)

6. *Final y*, if preceded by a *consonant*, is usually changed to *i* when a suffix is added which begins with a vowel (except the suffix *-ing*); as, happy, happiest, happiness; fly, flies; rely, reliance; accompany, accompaniment; very, verily; duty, dutiful. (Duteous, beauteous, and plenteous are not formed according to the rule.)

7. *Final y*, preceded by a *vowel*, or before the suffix *-ing*, is retained; as, valley, valleys; monkey, monkeys; spy, spying; pity, pitying.

APPENDIX IV

VERSES AND VERSE MAKING

SOME knowledge of versification is valuable for two reasons: it is an indispensable aid in the appreciative and musical reading of poetry, and the writing of verse is very excellent practice in the use of English. Merely for the skill it gives in choice and manipulation of words and the varied phrasing of sentences, it is an exercise that develops deftness, command of diction, and a nice ear for sound. It is therefore well worth while for a student occasionally to try his hand at verse making—taking care to see beforehand that he has something to say, and that he has a good model to follow in his versification.

The subject of prosody, or versification, is treated at some length in Maxwell's *Advanced Lessons in English Grammar* (pp. 306–318) and in most books on rhetoric. It includes the following divisions:—

1. *Meter,* or measuring of lines into portions called *feet.*

2. *Rhyme,* the agreement of the final syllables of lines in sound and accent. A correct rhyme consists in identity of accented vowel sounds, followed

244

by identical consonant sounds, and preceded by unlike consonant sounds.

Examples of correct rhyming : —

Battle, rattle; relate, state; range, strange; alley, valley; prodigious, religious; importunate, unfortunate.

Examples of incorrect or imperfect rhyming : —

(a) Corresponding syllables not accented alike; as, prel'ate, relate'; tak'ing, cling'; recline', i'odine.

(b) Sounds of vowels different; as, door, boor; care, far; river, never; disdain, amen; whistle, rustle; element, aliment.

(c) Vowels followed by unlike consonant sounds; as, cling-ing, singeing; wet, red; through, cough.

(d) Vowels preceded by like consonant sounds; as, scene, seen; restrain, strain; allay, delay; persuasion, dissuasion.

3. *Stanza-form*, or the grouping of lines into sets of a fixed number of lines, with a certain arrangement of rhymes. Examples of stanzas are the couplet, the triplet, the ballad stanza, the Spenserian stanza, the elegiac stanza, the rondeau, and the sonnet. Most of these are explained or exemplified later in this Appendix.

Of the above three divisions the first is the only one we shall consider at any length.

Meter. — Meter means measure. Poetry, like music, is divided into measures, each requiring the same amount of time. You can therefore beat time for verses just as for a piece of music. As in music ♩ ♩ has the same amount of time as ♩ · ♪ ♩ or ♩ ♩ ♩, so in poetry, three syllables may fill a measure having the same time allowance as one containing only two syllables. For example, take these lines from Lowell's *Vision of Sir Launfal* (the syllables that have the beat are marked with an accent):

> Down swépt the chill wínd from the móuntain peáks,
> From the snów five thóusand súmmers óld.

Each of these lines has four measures, or feet, as they are called; but in some cases there are three syllables to a foot, and in others only two. If we wished to represent the movement of these lines by musical characters, we should put: —

But since in every foot there is one syllable given more time than any other, the long syllables are usually represented by bars, and the short by curves, thus: —

This is less accurate than the representation by musical notes, but it is more convenient.

Sometimes the first syllables in the feet are the long ones. For example the nursery jingle: —

> Líttle Jack Hórner sát in a córner,
> Eáting his Chrístmas píe,

has a movement which may be represented thus: —

Here again we find feet of three syllables given the same time as feet of two syllables. (Beat time as you repeat the lines. The beat should fall on the long syllables.)

Kinds of feet. — The different kinds of feet are named according to the number of syllables they have, and the position of the accented or long syllables.

Feet of two syllables are either – ᴗ or ᴗ –.

Trochaic feet have the long syllable first, as in the words re'cent, moth'er, dif'fer, be'ing. The following are trochaic lines of verse : —

> Tell me not in mournful numbers,
> Life is but an empty dream. — LONGFELLOW.

Iambic feet have the long syllable second, as in the words combine', return', along', intent'. The following are iambic lines of verse : —

> You all did see that on the Lupercal
> I thrice presented him a kingly crown. — SHAKSPERE.

Feet of three syllables are either – ᴗ ᴗ or ᴗ ᴗ –.

Dactylic feet have the long syllable first, as in the words, syl'lable, clat'tering, cyl'inder, cel'ebrate. The following are dactylic lines of verse : —

> Cannon to right of them,
> Cannon to left of them. — TENNYSON.

Anapæstic feet have the long syllable last, as in the words, entertain', interfere', contradict', undertake'. The following are anapæstic lines of verse : —

The Assyrian came down like a wolf on the fold,
And his cohorts were gleaming with purple and gold.

— BYRON.

We have already seen in scanning (that is, marking off into their feet) the lines beginning, " Down swept the chill wind" and " Little Jack Horner," that *iambic and anapœstic* feet may easily be used in the same line, because they have the long syllable at the end of the foot; and that *trochaic and dactylic* feet may be used in the same line, because they both begin with the long syllable. In either case it is easy to read two short syllables in the time of one, just as in music two sixteenth notes may take the place of one eighth note.

For the sake, then, of simplicity, we may say that there are only *two types* of movement in English verse: the iambic (I am', I am', I am', etc.), and the trochaic (tro'chee, tro'chee, etc.); and in either kind two shorts may take the place of one, forming, in the iambic movement, an anapæstic foot, and, in the trochaic movement, a dactylic foot.

Kinds of lines, as to length.

1. Lines of one foot are called *monom'eter* lines. Examples : —

Iambic. — Away. (As in Herrick's *To Daffodils.*)
Anapœstic. — On a throne. (In Tennyson's *Merman.*)
Trochaic monometers may also be found, but lines of one foot are rare in any measure.

2. Lines of two feet are called *dim'eter*. Examples : —

Iambic. — The year's | last rose.
Trochaic. — Ori|ana
Anapœstic. — Of the mold|ering flow'rs.
Dactylic. — Take her up | tenderly.

3. Lines of three feet are called *trim'eter*. Examples : —

Iambic. — And I | desire | to rest.
Trochaic. — Neither | moon nor | starlight.
Anapœstic. — That he sings | in his boat | on the bay.
Dactylic. — Chasing each | other so | merrily.

4. Lines of four feet are called *tetram'eter*. Examples : —

Iambic. — A sec|ond voice | was at | mine ear.
Trochaic. — Then the | little | Hia watha.
Anapœstic. — Not a word | to each oth|er; we kept | the great pace.
Dactylic. — Brightest and | best of the | sons of the | morning.

5. Lines of five feet are called *pentam'eter*. Examples : —

Iambic. — And built | herself | an ev|erlast|ing name. (The iambic pentameter is the most used line in English poetry. It is sometimes called heroic verse. As we have seen, anapæstic feet may be substituted for one or more of the iambics in such a line.)
Trochaic and dactylic. — Over the | sea, with a | motion | slow and ar|rested.

6. Lines of six feet are called *hexam'eter*. Examples : —

Iambic. — As one | for knight|ly jousts | and fierce | encoun|-
    ters fit. (The iambic hexameter line is called
    an *Alexandrine*. See the dictionary.)
Dactylic. — This is the | forest pri|meval; the | murmuring
    | pines and the | hemlocks.

7. Lines of seven feet are called *heptam'eter*. Example : —

Iambic. — John Gil|pin was | a cit|izen | of cred|it and | re-
    nown. (Such lines are frequently divided into
    two lines, one tetrameter and the other trimeter.)

8. Lines of eight feet are called *octom'eter*. Example : —

Trochaic. — For the | mighty | wind a|rises, | roaring | sea-
    ward, | and I | go. (Octometers are rarely
    used, about the same effect being produced by
    two tetrameters.)

Rests. — As there are rests in music — measures
or parts of measures in which no notes are sounded
— so in poetry there are rests or pauses in the meter,
which must have their time allowed, even though no
syllables are uttered. In the following scansions the
letter *r* is used to mark a rest. If the accent or beat
falls upon a rest the *r* is italicized. The test of the
accuracy of the scanning of a line is whether the
syllables marked as long, or represented by a straight

line, really receive the stress or beat of the measure.
Beat time as in music : —

> (*a*) Sweet and low, sweet and low,
>   Wind of the western sea —
> Low, low, breathe and blow,
>   Wind of the western sea ! — TENNYSON.

Trochaic movement (4 feet, 3 feet, 4 feet, 3 feet) : —

$$
\begin{array}{llll}
- \;\cup & - (r) & - \;\cup & - (r) \\
- \cup\cup & - \;\cup & - (r) & \\
- \;(r) & - (r) & - \;\cup & - (r) \\
- \cup\cup & - \;\cup & - (r) &
\end{array}
$$

> (*b*) Break, break, break,
>   On thy cold gray stones, O sea !
> And I would that my tongue could utter
>   The thoughts that arise in me. — TENNYSON.

Iambic movement (3 feet, 3 feet, 4 feet, 3 feet) : —

$$
\begin{array}{llll}
(r) - & (r) - & (r) - & \\
\cup\cup - & \cup - & \cup - & \\
\cup\cup - & \cup\cup - & \cup - & \cup (r) \\
\cup - & \cup\cup - & \cup - &
\end{array}
$$

These selections also well illustrate how dactylic
feet may be used in the trochaic movement, and anapæstic feet in the iambic movement.

(*c*) The fine emphatic effect of the rest is also
shown in the following nursery jingle, especially in
the third line after " who " : —

> Ding, dong, bell,
>   Pussy's in the well ;
> Who put her in ?

Trochaic movement, 3 feet to a line : —

$$- \text{(r)} \mid - \text{(r)} \mid - \text{(r)}$$
$$- \cup \mid - \cup \mid - \text{(r)}$$
$$- \text{(r)} \mid - \cup \mid - \text{(r)}$$

Run-on lines. — It frequently happens that there is an extra syllable at the end of a line. In such a case this syllable is really a part of the first foot of the following line.

(*a*) Thus in the nursery jingle, —

> Old Mother Hubbard went to the cupboard
> To get her poor dog a bone ;
> When she got there, the cupboard was bare,
> And so the poor dog had none,

we have an iambic movement, beginning with a rest, the feet running 4, 3, 4, 3 : —

$$\text{(r)} - \mid \cup \cup - \mid \cup - \mid \cup \cup - \mid \cup$$
$$\cup - \mid \cup \cup - \mid \cup -$$
$$\text{(r)} - \mid \cup \cup - \mid \cup - \mid \cup \cup -$$
$$\cup - \mid \cup \cup - \mid \cup -$$

Here the extra syllable at the end of the first line clearly goes with the first foot of the following line, making the foot anapæstic. Note that the third line has no extra syllable at the end.

(*b*) This use of an extra end-syllable is common in Shakspere's later and better versification. For example, we have Hamlet's familiar lines : —

> To be, or not to be, that is the question:
> Whether 'tis nobler in the mind to suffer
> The slings and arrows of outrageous fortune,
> Or to take arms against a sea of troubles,
> And, by opposing, end them. To die ? To sleep.

Iambic movement, 5 feet to a line:

```
∪ — | ∪ — | ∪ — | ´∪ — | ∪ — | ∪
  — | ∪ ∪ — | ∪ — | ∪ — | ∪ — | ∪
∪ — | ∪ — | ∪ ∪̱ | ∪ — | ∪ — | ∪
  — | ∪ ∪ — | ∪ — | ∪ — | ∪ — | ∪
  — | ∪ ∪ — | ∪ — | ∪ ∪ — | ∪ — |
```

Here it will be observed that though the movement is iambic, the second, fourth, and fifth lines all begin with long or stressed syllables. The short syllables to fill out the iambic feet in these cases are found as extra syllables at the ends of the preceding lines. The first foot in the third line, for a similar reason, is an anapæstic foot, whose syllables are: -fer the slings, ∪ ∪ —·

There are illustrated in the last section two other points frequently exemplified in the best English poets.

(1) A short syllable is sometimes accented (´∪). Thus, in the first line quoted, the word " that " in the fourth foot is given the beat, as the natural emphasis, depending on the meaning of the words, requires "that" to be accented. But the regular beat in the foot falls on " is." Another example of a short syllable's being accented is in this line : —

Take these again, for to the noble mind.

∪ — | ∪ — | ´∪ ∪̱ | ∪ — | ∪ —

(2) The regular beat in a line may fall on a short syllable: Such a syllable may be represented by ∪̱.

Thus, the word " of," in the third line quoted, cannot be read as a long syllable, nor does it receive any emphasis. But it stands in the place of a long syllable, receiving the regular beat. In such a case give the syllable its full time in the measure, but do not in the least emphasize the short syllable, even though it comes in the place of a long syllable. The word " to " in the line last quoted is an example. Another example is the word " for " in this line : —

How does your honor for this many a day ?

ᴜ — | ᴜ — | ᴜ ᴜ | ᴜ — | ᴜ ᴜ — .

Or the word " the " in this : —

Is sicklied o'er with the pale cast of thought.

ᴜ — | ᴜ — | ᴜ ᴜ | ᴜ — | ᴜ —

Exercise 150. Scanning. — *Mark off in measures the syllables (and the rests, if any) in the following pieces of verse; also note the arrangement of the rhyming lines.*

1. The curfew tolls the knell of parting day,
    The lowing herd winds slowly o'er the lea,
    The plowman homeward plods his weary way,
    And leaves the world to darkness and to me.

(This is the opening stanza of Gray's *Elegy Written in a Country Churchyard*. This form of stanza is often called the *elegiac* stanza.)

2. And what is so rare as a day in June?
    Then, if ever, come perfect days;
    Then heaven tries the earth, if it be in tune,
    And over it softly her warm ear lays.
                — From LOWELL's *Vision of Sir Launfal.*

3. There was a time when meadow, grove, and stream,
    The earth, and every common sight
      To me did seem
     Appareled in celestial light,
 The glory and the freshness of a dream.
    It is not now as it hath been of yore;
      Turn wheresoe'er I may,
      By night or day,
The things which I have seen I now can see no more.
      —From WORDSWORTH's *Ode on Immortality.*

(An *ode* is a form of poem in which there is permitted much variety in length of lines and arrangement of rhymes.)

4. Lives of great men all remind us
    We can make our lives sublime,
  And, departing, leave behind us
    Footprints on the sands of time. — LONGFELLOW.

5. I had a little pony, his name was Dapple Gray;
I lent him to a lady, to ride a mile away.
She whipped him, she slashed him, and rode him through the mire:
I would not lend my pony now for all the lady's hire.
         — MOTHER GOOSE.

6. Little Tommy Tittlemouse
  Lived in a little house.
  He caught fishes
    In other men's ditches. — MOTHER GOOSE.

7. Sweet are the uses of adversity
  Which, like the toad, ugly and venomous,
  Wears yet a precious jewel in his head;
  And this our life, exempt from public haunt,
  Finds tongues in trees, books in the running brooks,
  Sermons in stones, and good in everything!
      — From SHAKSPERE's *As You Like It.*

(Verse that does not rhyme is called *blank verse.*)

8. There is a pleasure in the pathless woods,
There is a rapture on the lonely shore,
There is society where none intrudes,
By the deep sea, and music in its roar ;
I love not man the less, but nature more,
From these our interviews, in which I steal
From all I may be, or have been before,
To mingle with the universe, and feel
What I can ne'er express, yet cannot all conceal.

— From BYRON's Childe Harold.

(This stanza is an example of the *Spenserian* stanza, so called because it is that used in Edmund Spenser's great allegorical poem, *The Faerie Queene.* Note the arrangement of the rhymes, and the closing of the stanza with an Alexandrine, or six-foot line.)

Verse writing. — Most verses are simple and regular in movement and scansion, and as mere verses not hard to write. The easiest forms for the beginner to attempt are the following : —

(1) The *couplet* (two rhyming lines, each containing five feet, or each containing four feet). Examples : —

Pentameter couplets, *iambic :* —

But most by numbers judge a poet's song,
And smooth or rough, with them, is right or wrong.

— POPE.

Sir knight, though I have asked thy life, yet still
Thy destiny depends upon my will. — CHAUCER.

Tetrameter couplets, *iambic :* —

Disdains against its will to stay,
And struggles out, and flies away. — BUTLER.

Beneath her torn hat glowed the wealth
Of simple beauty and rustic health. — WHITTIER.

The train from out the castle drew,
But Marmion stopped to bid adieu. — SCOTT.

Tetrameter couplet, *trochaic:* —

Come, and trip it as you go,
On the light fantastic toe. — MILTON.

Exercise 151. Writing in couplets. — *The couplet being well adapted to descriptive and narrative verse, write the following jingles and verses in couplets.*

1. Complete the following nonsense couplets (tetrameter): —

Ten little kittens, ready to dine,
One choked on a bone, and then there were **nine**.
Nine little kittens ——
—— eight, etc.

2. Complete this alphabet jingle: —

A is an archer, steady and brave,
B is a barber, ready to shave,
C is a cormorant, greedy and strong,
D is a doctor whose bill is as long.

3. Write in four-foot couplets of trochaic movement, including dactylic feet if necessary, a comic anecdote, found in some book or newspaper, or any of the stories found on page 107.

4. Write in five-foot couplets of iambic movement an account of a picnic or an excursion. (If preferred, the iambic tetrameter couplet may be used, with anapæstic feet, introduced as desired.)

(2) The *ballad stanzas* of four lines are easy to write and pleasant to read. They are suited for lively narration and description. Examples : —

Iambic, 4, 3, 4, 3, rhyming second and fourth lines : —
　About, about, in reel and rout
　　The death fires danced at night ;
　The water, like a witch's oils,
　　Burnt green, and blue, and white. — COLERIDGE.

Iambic, 4, 4, 4, 4, rhyming second and fourth lines : —
　He was no sooner over the river,
　　Down in the forest to take the air,
　But eighty merchants of London city
　　Came kneeling before King Henry there.

　　　　　　　　　　　 — OLD BALLAD.

Exercise 152. Writing of ballad verse. — *Put into ballad verse the following little story :* —

The town rat and the country rat. — A town rat politely invited a country rat to dinner. They were to have some ripe old cheese and a well-cooked quail. The feast at last was spread out in a cozy corner, and merrily they set to eating; but hardly had they well begun, when a sudden racket at the door alarmed them, and they both scampered away as fast as they could. When the noise was over they returned: "Come," said the city rat, "let us finish our meal." — "Not a nibble more for me," said the rustic rat. "You come dine with me to-morrow, where all is quiet and safe. I am not envious of your life, for I have no love for pleasure when it is mixed with fear."

Exercise 153. Verse writing. — (*a*) *Put into ballad stanzas of either of the types mentioned above, the story of some book or tale you have recently read.*

(*b*) *Write jingles or verses in other stanza-forms, such as are exemplified in this Appendix or may be found elsewhere. These may be nonsense verses, or versified anecdotes, real or imaginary. Do not attempt any serious verse for some years to come (if ever).*

APPENDIX V

NOTES ON AUTHORS REFERRED TO OR QUOTED IN THIS BOOK

Joseph Addison, famous English writer of essays (and a few poems). 18th c. (1672–1719). The Spectator Papers (1711–1714).

Louisa M. Alcott, American story writer. Daughter of Bronson Alcott, a friend of Emerson. 19th c. (1831–1888). Little Women (1867).

James Lane Allen, American novelist (1849–   ). The Choir Invisible.

Francis Bacon, great English lawyer, statesman, philosopher, and essayist. 17th c. (1561–1626). Novum Organum, in Latin, 1620; Essays, in English (1597–1625).

Ballads, old narrative poems by unknown bards. Some manuscripts date back to the thirteenth and fourteenth centuries. A good convenient and interesting collection of them has been prepared by Professor F. B. Gummere, and published by Ginn & Co., Boston. The standard collection is that of Professor Child, 10 vols., Houghton, Mifflin & Co.

George Bancroft, American historian. 19th c. (1800–1891). History of the United States, 12 vols. (1854–1882).

William Black, English novelist (1841–1898). A Princess of Thule, Madcap Violet, etc.

R. D. Blackmore, English novelist. 19th c. (1825–1900). Lorna Doone.

James Boswell, famous for his Life of Samuel Johnson. 18th c. (1740–1795).

Charles Brockden Brown, the earliest American novelist. Late
18th c. (1771–1810). Wieland (1798); Arthur Mervyn
(1800).

Robert Browning, great English poet. 19th c. (1812–1890).
Plays, for example, A Blot in the 'Scutcheon; Colombe's
Birthday; Pippa Passes. Long poems: The Ring and the
Book; Sordello. Many much-loved short poems.

John Bunyan, English writer, famous for his Pilgrim's Progress.
17th c. (1628–1688).

Edmund Burke, great Irish orator and writer. 18th c. (1730–
1797). Speech on Conciliation with the American Colonies (1774); Inquiry into the Sublime and Beautiful
(1756).

Lord Byron, English poet. Early 19th c. (1788–1824). Trage-
dies. Narrative and descriptive poems: Childe Harold;
The Prisoner of Chillon. Lyric poems.

Thomas Campbell, Scottish poet. Early 19th c. (1777–1844).
The Pleasures of Hope (1798), and narrative poems.

Cervantes, famous Spanish novelist. 16th c. (1547–1616). Don
Quixote.

Geoffrey Chaucer, the first great English poet. 14th c. (1340–
1400). The Canterbury Tales; The Flower and the Leaf;
The House of Fame.

Samuel T. Coleridge, English poet and reflective writer. Early
19th c. (1772–1834). The Ancient Mariner (1798); several
other fine poems; many prose works.

James Fenimore Cooper, American romance writer. 19th c.
(1789–1851). Sea Tales: The Red Rover, etc. Indian
Tales: The Pathfinder; The Last of the Mohicans, etc.

William Cowper, English poet. 18th c. (1731–1800). Most of
his poems didactic. John Gilpin (1785) not in his usual
manner.

Richard Henry Dana, Jr., American writer. 19th c. (1815–
1882). Two Years before the Mast.

Charles Darwin, English scientist, one of the originators of the
theory of evolution. 19th c. (1809–1882). The Origin

of Species (1859); The Descent of Man; Movements of Plants; etc.

Richard Harding Davis, American story writer (1864–   ). Van Bibber and Other Stories.

Leonardo da Vinci, great Italian painter, architect, and scientist. 15th c. (1452–1519).

Daniel Defoe, English imaginative writer. Early 18th c. (1661–1731). Journal of the Plague; Robinson Crusoe (1719).

Thomas Dekker, minor dramatist of Shakspere's time. Early 17th c. (1570–1637?).

Charles Dickens, one of the most popular of English novelists. 19th c. (1812–1870). Pickwick Papers (1837); Nicholas Nickleby; Oliver Twist; Old Curiosity Shop; Dombey and Son; David Copperfield; Bleak House; Christmas Stories.

Edward Eggleston, American story writer and historian (1837–   ). The Circuit Rider; The Hoosier Schoolmaster; A History of the United States.

"George Eliot" (Mary Ann Evans, Mrs. Lewes, Mrs. Cross), the greatest English woman novelist. 19th c. (1819–1880). Scenes of Clerical Life; Adam Bede (1859); The Mill on the Floss; Silas Marner (1861); Romola; Felix Holt; Middlemarch; Daniel Deronda (1876); also essays and poems. The standard biography of George Eliot is by her husband, J. W. Cross.

Ralph Waldo Emerson, American reflective writer and poet. 19th c. (1803–1882). Nature (1836). Essays (1841–1844); Representative Men; English Traits; Conduct of Life. Poems: Concord Hymn; Woodnotes; May Day; The Problem.

Canon F. W. Farrar, English divine, and author of several theological and historical works (1831–   ).

Hamlin Garland, American story writer (1860–   ). (Subjects mostly western.) Main Traveled Roads.

Oliver Goldsmith, English writer of poems, prose, and plays. 18th c. (1728–1774). The Deserted Village; The Traveler; The Vicar of Wakefield; She Stoops to Conquer.

Nathaniel Hawthorne, greatest American romance writer. 19th c. (1804–1864). Twice-Told Tales (1837); The Scarlet Letter (1850); Mosses from an Old Manse; The House of the Seven Gables; The Blithedale Romance; Wonder Book for Boys and Girls; American Note Book; The Marble Faun.

William Hazlitt, English essayist and critic. Early 19th c. (1778–1830).

Oliver Wendell Holmes, American essayist, novelist, and poet. 19th c. (1809–1894). The Autocrat of the Breakfast Table (1858); The Professor at the Breakfast Table; The Poet at the Breakfast Table; Over the Teacups; One Hundred Days in Europe. Novels: Elsie Venner; The Guardian Angel. Among his poems: The Chambered Nautilus; Old Ironsides; The One Hoss Shay.

Victor Hugo, great French romance writer and poet. 19th c. (1802–1885). Les Miserables; Ninety-Three.

Washington Irving, perhaps the most classical of American writers. 19th c. (1783–1859). Knickerbocker's History of New York (1809); The Sketch Book; Bracebridge Hall; Tales of a Traveler; The Conquest of Granada; The Alhambra; Lives of Columbus, Mahomet, Goldsmith, and (1855) Washington.

G. P. R. James, English novelist. 19th c. (1801–1860).

Samuel Johnson, a great literary man of the eighteenth century in England (1709–1784). Poems; English Dictionary (1755); Rasselas (a tale); Tour of the Hebrides; The Rambler, The Idler (periodical essays); Lives of the Poets.

Rudyard Kipling, English poet and story writer (1865–   ). Plain Tales from the Hills (stories of life in India); The Phantom 'Rickshaw, and Other Tales; The Day's Work; Barrack Room Ballads and Other Poems; The Seven Seas.

Charles Lamb, one of the most gentle and delightful of English essayists. 19th c. (1775–1834). Essays of Elia. With his sister Mary he wrote Tales from Shakspere.

Henry W. Longfellow, the most popular of American poets. 19th c. (1807–1882). Two or three prose romances; Evangeline (1847); Golden Legend; Song of Hiawatha (1855); Courtship of Miles Standish; Tales of a Wayside Inn; Birds of Passage; many favorite short poems; Translation of Dante's Divina Commedia (1867).

James Russell Lowell, prominent American essayist, critic, and poet. 19th c. (1819–1891). Prose: Among my Books; My Study Windows; Fireside Travels; political and literary essays and addresses. Poems: The Biglow Papers (1848 and 1866); The Vision of Sir Launfal, (1848); Commemoration Ode (1865); Under the Willows; The Cathedral (1869). Some excellent short poems.

Thomas Babington Macaulay, famous English essayist, historian, and poet. 19th c. (1800–1859). Historical and literary essays; History of England, five vols.; Lays of Ancient Rome, and other poems.

John Milton, one of the greatest of English poets and prose writers. 17th c. (1608–1674). I. Early Poems: Hymn on the Nativity; Comus; Lycidas; L'Allegro; Il Penseroso. II. Prose works: Of Reformation; Of Education; On Divorce; Defense of the English People; Areopagitica. III. Later poems: Paradise Lost; Paradise Regained; Samson Agonistes; Sonnets.

Donald Grant Mitchell ("Ik Marvel"), an American imaginative writer and essayist (1822–   ). Reveries of a Bachelor; Dream Life; English Lands and Letters; American Lands and Letters.

Agnes Repplier, an American essayist (1855–   ). Varia, and other volumes of brief critical essays.

Dante Gabriel Rossetti, English painter and poet. 19th c. (1828–1882). Poems (1871), including The Blessed Damozel, Sister Helen, etc.; The Early Italian Poets (1873). His life and letters, edited by his brother, Wm. M. Rossetti, appeared in 1895.

John Ruskin, eloquent and influential writer (English) on art, ethics, and social economy (1819–1900). His works, collected in thirteen volumes, include Modern Painters, 1843–1860; Stones of Venice; Seven Lamps of Architecture; Ethics of the Dust; Sesame and Lilies; Time and Tide; Fors Clavigera; etc.

Sir Walter Scott, one of the greatest of novelists, and a poet. Early 19th c. (1771–1832). The Waverley Novels, mostly historical, including Waverley, The Monastery, The Abbot, Ivanhoe, Kenilworth, Quentin Durward, The Heart of Midlothian, Guy Mannering, The Bride of Lammermoor, and others almost as well known. His poems include The Lay of the Last Minstrel (1805), The Lady of the Lake (1810), and Marmion.

William Shakspere, the greatest of dramatic poets. Late 16th and early 17th c. (1564–1616). His plays are: (a) Historical: Henry IV, Henry V, Richard III, Richard II., King John. (b) Legendary: Hamlet, Lear, Macbeth, Cæsar, Antony and Cleopatra, Cymbeline. (c) Fictitious: Merchant of Venice, Midsummer Night's Dream, As You Like It, All's Well that Ends Well, Much Ado about Nothing, Othello, Winter's Tale, Tempest. Shakspere also wrote 154 sonnets and several other poems.

Robert Southey, English poet (laureate next before Wordsworth). 19th c. (1774–1843). His (prose) Life of Nelson is admirable.

Laurence Sterne, English novelist and preacher. 18th c. (1713–1768). A Sentimental Journey; Tristram Shandy; Sermons.

Robert Louis Stevenson, one of the most admired of recent English writers of fiction (1850–1894). Dr. Jekyll and Mr. Hyde; The Master of Ballantrae; David Balfour; Treasure Island; The New Arabian Nights. Will of the Mill; and other short stories. Essays: Familiar Studies of Men and Books; Virginibus Puerisque; Sketches and Criticisms. Note-books: An Inland Voyage; Travels with a Donkey. Poems: A Child's Garden of Verses.

Bayard Taylor, American writer of travels, poems, and novels. 19th c. (1825–1878). The Land of the Saracens; Views Afoot; Boys of Other Countries; Byways of Europe; Translation of "Faust"; Prince Deucalion; Poems of the Orient. Novels: Hannah Thurston; Story of Kennet.

Jeremy Taylor, English divine. 17th c. (1713–1767). Sermons; Holy Living; Holy Dying.

Alfred Tennyson, the most popular and one of the greatest of modern English poets. 19th c. (1809–1892). Longer poems: In Memoriam; Idyls of the King; The Princess; Maud; Enoch Arden. Dramas: Queen Mary; Harold; Becket. Many beautiful shorter poems.

Henry D. Thoreau, American naturalist and essayist. 19th c. (1817–1862). A Week on the Concord and Merrimac Rivers; Walden; The Maine Woods; Cape Cod; Summer; Winter.

Mrs. Humphry Ward, noted English woman novelist (1851–). Robert Elsmere; David Grieve; Marcella; The Story of Bessie Costrell.

Daniel Webster, the greatest American orator. 19th c. (1782–1852). Eulogy on Adams and Jefferson; Bunker Hill Orations; Speech in Reply to Hayne (1829); Speech on the Murder of Captain White.

Walt Whitman, regarded by some as one of the greatest of American poets and writers of prose. 19th c. (1819–1892). Poems all included under the title, Leaves of Grass. His prose includes: Collect; Democratic Vistas; Specimen Days in America; The Wound Dresser.

John Greenleaf Whittier, a well-known American writer of ballads and other poems. 19th c. (1807–1892). Maud Muller; The Barefoot Boy; Barbara Frietchie; Snowbound; Among the Hills. Many favorite short poems.

Kate Douglas Wiggin (Mrs. Riggs), American writer of juvenile stories and other books (1857–). The Birds' Christmas Carol; The Story of Patsy; Children's Rights; A Cathedral Courtship; A Summer in Southern California.

INDEX

Accent in verse, 246, 248.
Accuracy in use of words, 188–191, 199–203.
Adjectives, suggestive use of, 203–205.
Allegory, 185.
Ailiteration, 185.
Anapæstic feet, 247.
" And " habit, 54–56.
" And which," 192.
Antithesis, 151.
Apostrophe, uses of, 239.
Argument, defined, 13, 16.
  lists of subjects, 16.
  general treatment, 209–215.
Arrangement, grammatical, 149, 197.
  for clearness, 117–120.
  for emphasis, 149–155.
Article, omission of, 114.
Authors, notes on, 259–266.

Balance in sentences, 151, 152.
Ballad stanzas, 257.
Blank verse, 255.
Briefs in argument, 212–214.
Business letters, 170–174.

Capitals, rules for, 240, 241.
Cases of pronouns, 194, 195.
Change of subject, faulty, 56.
Characters in narratives, 102.
Chaucer, 222.
Choice of subjects, 111.
Choice of words, for accuracy, 188–191, 198–203.
  for emphasis, 156–159.
  for suggestion, 203–205.
Clauses, 76.
Clearness, 111–120.
Climax, 153.
Colon, uses of, 238.

Colors in description, 65.
Comma, uses of, 234, 235.
Comparisons, in description, 62, 63.
  and contrasts in paragraphs, 128–132.
Completeness, in compositions, 18.
  in paragraphs, 40.
  in sentences, 57, 113–115, 197, 198.
Complex sentences, 79, 81, 84–88.
Composition, purpose of, 9–11.
  kinds, 12–16.
  general principles of, 18.
Composition books, 11, 36.
Compound sentences, 80–83.
Conjunctions, kinds, 85.
  with relatives, 192.
Contents of descriptions, 17–20, 25.
  of expositions, 207.
  of paragraphs, 121–142.
Correctness, in diction, 187, 188.
  in syntax, 57, 113, 192–198.
Couplets in verse, 256.
Creasy, 63.
Criticism, of a composition, 36, 176, 215.
  scheme of marks for, 217–220.

Dactylic feet, 247.
Dash, uses of, 236.
Debate, 209–215.
Denying the opposite in sentences, 157, 158.
  in argument, 209, 210.
Description, defined, 12, 15.
  general treatment, 17–36, 60–74.
  lists of subjects, 15.
Details, in description, 24, 25, 60.
  or particulars in paragraphs, 122–124.
Direct narration, 147, 148, 166.

Effects, statement of, in description, 64.
or results, in paragraphs, 132-134.
Elegiac stanza, 254.
Elements of sentences, 75-77.
Emphasis, 143-161.
English language, brief history of, 221-229.
Evangeline, 91.
Exclamatory sentences, 145, 146, 161.
Expositions, defined, 13, 16.
lists of subjects, 16.
general treatment, 206-208.

Feet, kinds of, in poetry, 247, 248.
Figures of speech, 177-186.
Formal notes, 163.
Franklin, 99.
French element in English speech, 221-223, 226.

Glance in description, 24, 25.
Grammatical agreement, of verbs, 195.
of pronouns, 194.
Greek element in English, 222-225, 229.

Headings, in letters, 165.
Homer, 64.
Hugo, 62.
Hyphen, uses of, 239.

Iambic feet, 247.
Iambic movement, 248.
Imitation, 23, etc.
Indention, 37, 41.
Indirect and direct narration, 147, 148, 160.
Infinitive, splitting of, 197.
Informal notes and letters, 164-169.
Instances or examples in paragraphs, 125-127.
Interestingness, 10, 101-103.
Interrogation, 144-146, 161.
Introduction in description, 25.
Inversion, 149, 150.

John Gilpin's Ride, 93.

Latin elements in English, 222, 226, 228.
Letters, parts of, 165-168.

Letter writing, 162-176.
Lincoln, 92.
Lines in verse, kinds of, 248-250.
Longfellow, 91, 93.
Loose sentences, 154.

Merchant of Venice, 93.
Metaphor, 181-183.
Meter, 244-248.
Metonymy, 184.
Milton, 91.

Narration, defined, 12, 15.
lists of subjects, 15.
general treatment, 90-110.
use of "direct narration," 147, 148, 160.

Omissions in sentences, 57, 113-115.
"Only," position of, 118.
Onomatopoeia, 186.
Outlining, importance of, 24, 40, 41.
in description, 20, 25-29.
narration, 90-93.
in exposition, 207, 208.
in argument, 210-214.

Paragraphs, defined, 37.
general treatment, 37-51, 121-142.
contents of, 121-142.
topics of, 37.
Parentheses, 235.
Participles, position of, 118.
Paul Revere's Ride outlined, 99.
Periods, uses of, 232.
Periodic sentences, 154.
Perry's Victory, 106.
Personification, 183, 184.
Phrases, 76-78.
Plan, importance, in composition, 18.
in description, 24, 25.
Plot in narratives, 102, 103.
Poems for outlining, 100.
Point of view in description, 60-62.
Position, for emphasis in sentences, 149.
of modifiers, 117-120, 197.
Possessive case, use of, 193.
punctuation of, 239.
Precision in use of words, 188-191, 199-203.
Prefixes, 227

Pronouns, obscure in sentences, 115.
agreement with antecedents, 194.
relatives, use of, 86, 189-191.
Proofs, kinds of, 211, 212.
strength of, 211.
Punctuation, 23, 232-240.

Question mark, 233.
Quotation marks, uses of, 236.

Reasons or causes in paragraphs, 134.
Redundancy, 156.
Refutation, 210.
Relative pronouns, use of, 86.
restrictive and coördinate, 189-191.
preceded by conjunctions, 192.
Repetition, 156, 157.
Rests in verse, 250.
Rhyme, 244.
Rip Van Winkle outlined, 92.
Run-on lines in verse, 252.

Salutations in letters, 164.
Saxon element in English, 221, 225.
Scale in description, 61.
Scanning, 248, 254.
Scott, a walk with, 124.
Selection in composition, 18, 20.
Semicolon, uses of, 237, 238.
Sense impressions in description, 65-72.
Sentences, grammatical kinds, 78-88.
balanced, 151, 152.
loose, 154.
periodic, 154.
inverted, 149, 150.
Setting or scene in narration, 102.
Shakspere, life of, 93.
" Shall " and " will," 189, 191.
Simile, 177-181.
Simple sentences, 78, 83.
Smoothness in paragraphs, 121.

Specific words, 158, 159.
Spelling, rules for, 241-243.
Spenserian stanza, 256.
Sphinx, the, 104.
Stanza forms, 245.
Style, as affected by derivation, 230, 231.
in narration, 102.
Suffixes, 228.
Suggestion in words, 203-205.
Superscription of a letter, 167-169.
Suspended or periodic sentences, 154, 155.
Synecdoche, 185.
Synonyms, 199-201.
Syntax, correctness in, 57, 113, 192-198.

" That," use of, 190.
Titles in letters, 167, 168.
Topic sentences, 43.
Topics of paragraphs, 37.
Transformation, of elements, 77, 83.
of sentences, 80-90.
Trochaic feet, 247.
Trochaic movement, 248.

Underscoring, 240.
Unity, in compositions, 18.
in paragraphs, 40.
in sentences, 53-59, 112.
Use of words, accurate, 188-191.
suggestive, 203-205.

Verbs, grammar of, 195, 196.
Verses and verse making, 244-258.

" Which " habit, 116.
" Will " and " shall," 189, 191.
Word coinage, 229.
Word formation, 227-229.
Words, sources of English, 221-225.

TYPOGRAPHY BY J. S. CUSHING & CO., NORWOOD, MASS.

Eclectic English Classics

Arnold's (Matthew) Sohrab and Rustum	$0.20
Burke's Conciliation with the American Colonies	.20
Burns's Poems—Selections	.20
Byron's Poems—Selections	.25
Carlyle's Essay on Robert Burns	.20
Chaucer's Canterbury Tales—Prologue and Knighte's Tale	.25
Coleridge's Rime of the Ancient Mariner	.20
Cooper's Pilot	.40
Defoe's History of the Plague in London	.40
DeQuincey's Revolt of the Tartars	.20
Dryden's Palamon and Arcite	.20
Emerson's American Scholar, Self Reliance, and Compensation	.20
Franklin's Autobiography	.35
George Eliot's Silas Marner	.30
Goldsmith's Vicar of Wakefield	.35
Gray's Poems—Selections	.20
Irving's Sketch Book—Selections	.20
Irving's Tales of a Traveler	.50
Macaulay's Second Essay on Chatham	.20
Macaulay's Essay on Milton	.20
Macaulay's Essay on Addison	.20
Macaulay's Life of Samuel Johnson	.20
Milton's L'Allegro, Il Penseroso, Comus, and Lycidas	.20
Milton's Paradise Lost—Books I and II	.20
Pope's Homer's Iliad, Books I, VI, XXII, and XXIV	.20
Pope's Rape of the Lock, and Essay on Man	.20
Scott's Ivanhoe	.50
Scott's Marmion	.40
Scott's Lady of the Lake	.30
Scott's The Abbot	.60
Scott's Woodstock	.60
Shakespeare's Julius Caesar	.20
Shakespeare's Twelfth Night	.20
Shakespeare's Merchant of Venice	.20
Shakespeare's Midsummer-Night's Dream	.20
Shakespeare's As You Like It	.20
Shakespeare's Macbeth	.20
Shakespeare's Hamlet	.25
Sir Roger de Coverley Papers (The Spectator)	.20
Southey's Life of Nelson	.40
Tennyson's Princess	.20
Tennyson's Idylls of the King—Selections	.20
Webster's Bunker Hill Orations	.20
Wordsworth's Poems—Selections	.20

Copies sent, prepaid, to any address on receipt of the price.

American Book Company

New York • Cincinnati • Chicago

Text-Books in Grammar for Advanced Grades

BASKERVILL AND SEWELL'S ENGLISH GRAMMAR . 90 cents

An advanced grammar for use in High School, Academy and College classes. It combines in a remarkable degree a clear and concise statement of the facts of the language, based on its reputable use in literature, with rational methods for teaching and applying the same. The treatment includes Parts of Speech, Analysis, and Syntax, each part separate and distinct, but so articulated into the others as to make a complete, systematic, and harmonious whole.

LYTE'S ADVANCED GRAMMAR AND COMPOSITION . 75 cents

For use in High Schools, Normal Schools, and other Preparatory Schools. Based on the author's popular "Grammar and Composition" and embodying the improvements suggested by successful class room work. The general plan of the work and the development of the subject are in strict accordance with accepted pedagogical principles.

MAXWELL'S ADVANCED LESSONS IN ENGLISH GRAMMAR . 60 cents

For use in Higher Grammar Grades and High Schools. It embraces all the theory and practice necessary during the last two years of a grammar school course or throughout a high school course. It is intended to serve two purposes ;—first, as a *text-book*, supplying the principles and rules of the science as well as their applications, and second, as a *book of reference*, to be used whenever difficulties are presented either in the student's own compositions, or in literature that is subjected to critical study.

POWELL AND CONNOLLY'S RATIONAL GRAMMAR OF THE ENGLISH LANGUAGE . . . . . . 60 cents

This new grammar differs widely in treatment and terminology from other text-books in English. The subject is developed logically, and every point is made simple and clear. The practical side of the study— the correct use of language in speech and writing — is especially emphasized.

Copies of any of these books will be sent, prepaid, to any address on receipt of the price.

American Book Company

New York   •   Cincinnati   •   Chicago

Webster's School Dictionaries
REVISED EDITIONS

WEBSTER'S SCHOOL DICTIONARIES in their revised form constitute a progressive series, carefully graded and especially adapted for Primary Schools, Common Schools, High Schools, Academies, and private students. These Dictionaries have all been thoroughly revised, entirely reset, and made to conform in all essential respects to that great standard authority in English,—Webster's International Dictionary.

WEBSTER'S PRIMARY SCHOOL DICTIONARY .   .   . $0.48

Containing over 20,000 words and meanings, with over 400 illustrations.

WEBSTER'S COMMON SCHOOL DICTIONARY .   .   . $0.72

Containing over 25,000 words and meanings, with over 500 illustrations.

WEBSTER'S HIGH SCHOOL DICTIONARY $0.98

Containing about 37,000 words and definitions, and an appendix giving a pronouncing vocabulary of Biblical, Classical, Mythological, Historical, and Geographical proper names, with over 800 illustrations.

WEBSTER'S ACADEMIC DICTIONARY. Cloth, $1.50; Indexed, $1.80

The Same .   .   .   . Half Calf, $2.75; Indexed, $3.00

Abridged directly from the International Dictionary, and giving the orthography, pronunciations, definitions, and synonyms of the large vocabulary of words in common use, with an appendix containing various useful tables, with over 800 illustrations.

SPECIAL EDITIONS

Webster's Countinghouse Dictionary . . Sheep, Indexed,		$2.40
Webster's Condensed Dictionary . Cloth, $1.44; Indexed,		1 75
The Same . . . Half Calf, $2.75; Indexed,		3.00
Webster's Handy Dictionary		.15
Webster's Pocket Dictionary. Cloth		.57
The Same. Roan Flexible		.69
The Same. Roan Tucks		.78
The Same. Morocco, Indexed		.90
Webster's American People's Dictionary and Manual . .		.48
Webster's Practical Dictionary		.80

Copies of any of Webster's Dictionaries will be sent, prepaid, to any address on receipt of the price by the Publishers:

American Book Company

New York   •   Cincinnati   •   Chicago

(1c4)

Made in the USA
Middletown, DE
20 September 2021

48694106R00156